Reading Rivers in Roman Literature and Culture

Roman Studies: Interdisciplinary Approaches

Sarolta A. Takács, Rutgers University, Editor

Editorial Board
Miriam Carlisle, Washington and Lee College, Associate Editor
Mary Ebbot, College of the Holy Cross, Assistant Editor
Ellen Perry, College of the Holy Cross, Assistant Editor
Werner Riess, University of North Carolina, Chapel Hill, Assistant Editor
Casey Dué Hackett, University of Houston, Liaison with Greek Studies

As did their cultures in antiquity, Greek Studies and Roman Studies will complement each other. Roman Studies will focus on subjects related to the Roman world, examined from a multitude of angles. As the chronological, the territorial, and the cultural expanse of the field demand interdisciplinarity, this series encourages the implementation of newer disciplines and methodologies, such as anthropology, linguistics, sociology, and literary theory, alongside the established methodologies of archaeology and philology. The series editors for Roman Studies: Interdisciplinary Approaches encourage new and alternative approaches, especially from younger scholars whose work bridges more than one discipline and encourages us to think beyond established patterns and models of explanation.

Reading Rivers in Roman Literature and Culture, by Prudence J. Jones

Reading Rivers in Roman Literature and Culture

Prudence J. Jones

LEXINGTON BOOKS

A Division of
ROWMAN & LITTLEFIELD PUBLISHERS, INC.
Lanham • Boulder • New York • Toronto • Oxford

LEXINGTON BOOKS

A division of Rowman & Littlefield Publishers, Inc.
A wholly owned subsidiary of The Rowman & Littlefield Publishing Group, Inc.
4501 Forbes Boulevard, Suite 200
Lanham, MD 20706

PO Box 317
Oxford
OX2 9RU, UK

1006473953

British Library Cataloguing in Publication Information Available

Library of Congress Cataloging-in-Publication Data

Jones, Prudence J., 1971–
Reading rivers in Roman literature and culture / Prudence J. Jones.
    p. cm.
Includes bibliographical references and index.
ISBN 0-7391-1108-6 (alk. paper)—ISBN 0-7391-1240-6 (pbk. : alk. paper)
 1. Latin literature—History and criticism. 2. Rivers in literature. 3. Geography,
Ancient, in literature. 4. Virgil—Knowledge—Geography. 5. Nature in literature.
6. Rivers—Rome. I. Title.
PA6029.N4.J66 2005
870.9'321693—dc22   2005016166

Printed in the United States of America

♾™ The paper used in this publication meets the minimum requirements of American
National Standard for Information Sciences—Permanence of Paper for Printed Library
Materials, ANSI/NISO Z39.48–1992.

For my parents

Contents

Foreword

Sarolta A. Takács, Editor

With the introduction of this series, *Roman Studies: Interdisciplinary Approaches,* we hope to enhance understanding of the ancient Roman world. This empire was multicultural and lasted, from a mythological foundation to the fall of Constantinople, over two millennia. Even its political demise in 1453 did not spell the end of long established traditions. New nations, new empires developed on the vast territory that was once the Roman Empire. All of these countries defined themselves vis-à-vis Roman political and legal traditions as well as Greco-Roman culture. The chronological, the territorial, and the cultural expanse demand interdisciplinary examination. In this series we hope to encourage the employment of new methodologies as they emerge from both established and emerging disciplines.

Reading Rivers in Roman Literature and Culture, by Prudence Jones, examines how rivers function as poetic devices in Roman literature, in particular, in Vergil's *Aeneid.* Before embarking on an exploration of the narrative possibilities of rivers, Jones explores the cultural background. This exploration shows that rivers function as definition points, which help shape an understanding of the literary world. In part 1, Jones's focus is on the symbolic role of a river; the role that links a river to cosmology, ritual, and ethnography. The defining qualities of a river, movement and directionality, are also those of a text. In part 2, Jones shows how Vergil used a river, and its flowing, as a narratological device. She also directs our view to visual narratives like the Palestrina Nile Mosaic where the river connects the present to the past. Jones's study beautifully establishes how, for Vergil, a river is not just a setting but an opportunity for self-reference and a mediator between poetry and poet. What Vergil established continues to this date.

Preface

This book began as a Harvard University dissertation, the topic of which was inspired by my study of Vergil with Richard Thomas and of ancient geography with Christopher Jones. When rivers seemed to be the natural intersection of these two topics, I began to examine their literary contexts more closely. James Romm's book, *The Edges of the Earth in Ancient Thought*, led me to believe that rivers not only formed a logical category, but also that careful study of one geographical feature might yield a more general understanding of the way the ancients viewed their world.

Although my research began with an extensive catalogue of passages in which rivers received mention, I was drawn again and again to Vergil and to the tendency of rivers in his poems to break the bounds of landscape and interact with the text itself. In the end, this has become the focus of the book. This literary phenomenon, however, exists in the context of (and, indeed, because of) the role river water plays in Greco-Roman society. This fact necessitates an examination of the cultural meaning of rivers, a task that has led me to much fascinating research on cosmology, ritual, and ethnography.

I hope that this study will not only be of use to those who study landscape or Vergil, but also that it will prompt further investigation of rivers as a motif in the writings of other Greek and Latin authors, as well as the study of other significant geographical features. Translations are my own, except where noted.

I would like to thank Richard Thomas, Richard Tarrant, Christopher Jones, Sarolta Takács, Gregory Nagy, Gloria Ferrari, Kathleen Coleman, Mary Lefkowitz, Hugh Lloyd-Jones, Jean Turfa, Rolf Schneider, Kathryn Slanski, Thomas Jenkins, and Mark Schiefsky.

Introduction

This study examines rivers as a literary phenomenon, particularly in the poetry of Vergil. The point of such an investigation is twofold: an examination of Vergil's poetry elucidates particularly clearly a point about rivers (that their inclusion functions almost as a literary device) and an examination of rivers makes a point about Vergil (that rivers are essential to understanding the trajectory of his works, in particular the structure of the *Aeneid*). This study does not aim to be comprehensive; to include every reference to rivers in Roman literature would not only produce a multivolume work, but also would obscure the argument, which concerns just one aspect of the river as a symbol.

This study depends primarily on the close analysis of the poetry of Vergil and of other relevant authors. Certain pieces of material culture also serve as evidence. Before embarking on a detailed investigation of the role rivers play in a literary environment, some cultural background is needed. Thus, part 1 examines the Greco-Roman understanding of the river in its primary symbolic roles: cosmological, ritual, and ethnographical. This overview brings together Greek and Roman examples to ascertain the essential meaning of rivers in the ancient world and to elucidate the characteristics of the river that persist over a period of centuries.

Part 2 analyzes the river as a literary device, with particular attention to the works of Vergil, and argues that descriptions of rivers in Roman poetry are, in many cases, a form of authorial comment on the progress or structure of a narrative. In addition to being a common metaphor for poetic speech, rivers function topographically in a way that supports this connection. As a dynamic and changeable part of the landscape, rivers are uniquely able to interact with the dynamics of poetry. The defining qualities of a river are motion and directionality. This directional motion is analogous to a text, whether seen in terms of the author's inspiration or the reader's experience. Thus, the river itself represents the independently existing narrative in which author and reader may participate within certain established parameters. Unlike a road, which exists as a static object along which people can move equally well in either direction, a river normally has a predetermined direction associated with it ("normally" because rivers, particularly in literature, can behave in unusual ways, stopping their current or even flowing backwards, both situations that can have metatextual significance).

Callimachus's *Peri Potamon* may be partly to thank for the increased association of poetry and rivers found in Roman literature. Perhaps this repository of rivers provided more than an encyclopedia of streams for subsequent versification: perhaps it also motivated an increased association between water and words. Yet it is not only texts that employ rivers in a self-referential context. Visual narratives of the Roman period demonstrate some of the same principles when it comes to watercourses. In particular, the Palestrina Nile Mosaic and Trajan's Column showcase some of the same narrative techniques as the poetry of Vergil, Ovid, and others.

Vergil is the first classical author to fully exploit the narrative possibilities of the river and, as such, makes a lasting impression on the way rivers function in subsequent literature. In the *Eclogues*, *Georgics*, and *Aeneid*, the river represents Vergil's vision of his own storytelling. At this point, a brief summary of the way rivers (and flowing water generally) function in the works of Vergil will be helpful.

In the *Eclogues*, water and poetry are the two essential elements of the pastoral scene: both represent life for the characters in those poems. When they lose a poetic voice they lose life as surely as if they were deprived of water. The very structure of the collection reinforces the central role of water. The first and last mentions of rivers or springs come at the midpoint of the first and last *Eclogues* (1.39 and 10.42). Both passages concern the ability of a well-watered *locus amoenus* to compensate for loss, a theme central to the *Eclogues*.

The *Georgics* contains Vergil's most emphatic statement on water and the poet. In the case of Orpheus, water even has the power to sustain the voice of a poet no longer in one piece. In the *Georgics*, however, the poet is juxtaposed with the farmer, who uses water in quite a different way, but finds it no less essential to survival. Water is one image that links the world of agriculture with the realm of the poet.

The symbolism of rivers pervades the *Aeneid* in particular. The *Aeneid* is a journey and in that spatial, temporal, and literary journey the river is the perfect emblem for the directional progress that journey implies. In a sense, however, the *Aeneid*'s journey is circular, and the concept of the round river, which has an antecedent in Homer, can encompass that sort of equivocal closure.

The works of Vergil will not provide the structuring principle to part 2, however. Rather, the organization will be thematic. Nevertheless, the themes considered map roughly onto Vergil's three major works. Thus, the section on rivers and poetic speech draws much of its evidence from the *Eclogues*, the section on river catalogues has as its focal point the *Georgics*, and the discussions of round rivers and upstream voyages apply primarily to the *Aeneid*. A section on the *Nachleben* of river motifs indicates the influence Vergil, along with Greco-Roman cultural notions of water, has had upon subsequent authors.

Abbreviations

LIMC   *Lexicon Iconographicum Mythologiae Classicae.* Zurich: Artemis, 1981-1999.

LSJ   H. G. Liddell and R. Scott, *Greek-English Lexicon,* revised by H. S. Jones, edited by P. G. W. Glare. New York: Oxford University Press, 1996.

OCD   *The Oxford Classical Dictionary,* edited by S. Hornblower and A. Spawforth. New York: Oxford University Press, 1996.

OLD   *Oxford Latin Dictionary,* edited by P. G. W. Glare. New York: Oxford University Press, 1996.

Part I

The Cultural Meaning of Rivers
in Greece and Rome

Chapter One

Cosmology

The essential symbolic meanings of rivers for Greco-Roman society are important for any investigation of their literary significance. In this section, I will explore the primary ways in which rivers function on a symbolic level. Rivers, along with other aspects of the physical surroundings, influence the societies that inhabit those surroundings. As Shils notes, society has a structure that reflects and goes beyond geography. A society has a center that has a fixed location within the space occupied by that society. The true significance of the center, however, lies in its symbolic association with the unifying principles of the society. In this way, a feature based in geography takes on a key role in determining the character of a society. Shils sums up this connection with the maxim *cuius regio, eius religio*, thus acknowledging the influence place can have on beliefs and identity.[1]

Rivers behave in a similar way: they interact with several key concepts through which the Greeks and Romans construct and understand their world: cosmology, ritual, and ethnography. In these contexts, rivers contribute to defining personal identity with respect to one's immediate society (ethnography), to the gods (ritual), and to one's temporal position within the universe (cosmology). Thus, rivers provide a means of translating abstract ideas about the physical, metaphysical, and temporal structure of the world into a concrete and comprehensible framework. In both Greek and Roman societies, rivers were important in myth and ritual and, thus, their symbolic value has deep cultural roots. For this reason, the river lends itself well to being a literary motif. As we shall see in part 2, artists and authors, particularly in the Hellenistic and Roman periods, employ rivers in developing a kind of textual geography that enables them to draw attention to the text as well as its subject. For this reason, a familiarity with the cultural roles of rivers will provide a basis for understanding their role in conceptions of artistic creation.

Cosmogonies, whether they involve the genealogy of anthropomorphic entities or the physical transformation of inanimate substances, seek to account for the world we see and envision its origins. As such, they must offer a starting

---

1. Shils 1975, 3.

point and a process of development. In Near Eastern, Egyptian, and Mediterranean cosmogonies, water plays a significant role, usually as an originative substance. An originative substance must contain within itself the potential to produce all other materials. One possible explanation for the attractiveness of water
to this role is its ability to alter its form.[2] Water has observable properties that
suggest this notion of mutability. Water adopts the shape of any container into
which it is poured and all three of its phases (solid, liquid, and gas) exist at easily achievable temperatures. These phenomena may have suggested that water
contains within itself other forms. Additionally, water is a prerequisite for and a
necessity of human life.[3] It is a logical conclusion, then, that water preceded life
on earth and that it contributed to the development of observable life forms.

For these reasons, we might expect water to be present at the beginning of
ancient cosmogonies and to possess the ability to produce other materials. Indeed, this is the evidence we find. In both genealogical and physical cosmogonies, water is essential. Early cosmogonies tend to be genealogical, assigning the
tasks of creating the universe to anthropomorphic divine powers that represent
natural forces.

The Egyptian creation story begins with Nun, the primordial waters, identified as groundwater.[4] A prayer to Amun describes that god as the eldest of the
gods and as a creator, but also as originating from Nun:

> An offering given by the king (to) Amun,
> Lord of the Thrones-of-the-Two-Lands,
> King of eternity, lord of everlastingness,
> Ruler, lord of the two great plumes,
> Sole one, primordial, eldest,
> Primeval, without [equal],
> [Creator] of men and gods,
> Living flame that came from Nun,
> Maker of light for mankind;
>
>   ("The Prayer for Offerings")[5]

The god Re, referred to as "the self-created," also originates in Nun:

> It happened [in the time of the majesty of] Re, the self-created, after he had be-
> come king of men and gods together: Mankind plotted against him, while his
> majesty had grown old, his bones being silver, his flesh gold, his hair true lapis
> lazuli. When his majesty perceived the plotting of mankind against him, his
> majesty said to his followers: "Summon to me my Eye, and Shu, Tefnut, Geb,
> Nut, and the fathers and mothers who were with me when I was in Nun, and

---

2. Indeed, this is a primary role of water in myth (Ninck 1921, 138-80).
3. As a substance that comprises 67 percent of the human body, water is a physical necessity.
Without it, a human life will be lost within a few days (Haslam 1991, 1). A supply of water, therefore, is an immediate necessity for any society (Squatriti 1998, 1).
4. Lichtheim 1976, 47 n. 11.
5. Translation by Lichtheim 1976, 16.

also the god Nun;"

("The Destruction of Mankind")[6]

The primordial water, then, not only precedes everything else in the universe, but also acts as the site of creation even for the self-created. As we shall see, this role is similar to that of Okeanos in Greek cosmology: Okeanos is a primordial figure and also possesses an ongoing generative power.

The idea that life arises from the waters resembles the agricultural fertility that resulted from the annual inundation of the Nile.[7] This idea is expressed particularly clearly in the worship of Isis.

By extrapolating an annual change, the Egyptians could understand a massive transformation in terms of a smaller process with which they were familiar and which involved forces known to exist in their immediate surroundings. For those living on the banks of the Nile, water was the major force that reshaped the landscape in a dramatic and easily observable way and, thus, must have seemed the most probable force responsible for creating the entire world.

In Mesopotamia, too, rivers dominated the landscape: the Tigris and the Euphrates, like the Nile, represent a creative power from which life originates. The observable silting process probably influenced theories of the origin of the universe.[8] Several Mesopotamian cosmogonies accord water a prominent role in the process. Apsu and Tiamat may be envisioned as mixing their waters together as they engage in the act of creation:

> When skies above were not yet named,
> Nor earth below pronounced by name,
> Apsu, the first one, their begetter,
> And maker Tiamat, who bore them all,
> Had mixed their waters together,
> But had not formed pastures, nor discovered reed-beds;
> When yet no gods were manifest,
> Nor names pronounced, nor destinies decreed,
> Then gods were born within them.

(*The Epic of Creation*, Tablet 1)[9]

Later in the same tablet, Mother Hubur (river) is referred to as a creator:

> Mother Hubur, who fashions all things,
> Contributed an unfaceable weapon: she bore giant snakes,

(*The Epic of Creation*, Tablet 1)[10]

---

6. Translation by Lichtheim 1976, 198.
7. Frankfort et al. 1967, 50.
8. Heidel 1951, 61.
9. Translation by Dalley 1991, 233.
10. Translation by Dalley 1991, 237.

As the preceding passages demonstrate, divinities associated with water contain within themselves the power to create as well as the elements from which other substances are made.[11] Water itself may have a creative force as well:

> After Anu had created the heaven,
> (And) the heaven had created the earth,
> (And) the earth had created the rivers,
> (And) the rivers had created the canals,
> (And) the canals had created the morass,
> (And) the morass had created the worm,
> The worm came weeping before Shamash,
> His tears flowing before Ea.
>
> ("The Worm and the Toothache" 1-8)[12]

This system of descent links earthly beings with the gods via the mediation of water.[13]

Early Greek thought also expresses the relationship between water and the results of its productivity in terms of genealogy. In Homer, the river god Okeanos is the father of all the gods (*Iliad* 14.200-202) and in Hesiod, he is the parent of divinities representing the waters of the earth, the river gods, and naiads (*Theogony* 337-48). Although the Hesiodic cosmogony begins with Chaos rather than primeval waters, it is possible either that a cosmogony involving primordial water coexisted or that Chaos can be understood as an idea similar to originative water. Indeed, there is some evidence of alternatives to the Hesiodic cosmogony: Rudhardt cites Hieronymus and Hellanicus as sources for a cosmogony in which the two first principles earth and water produce a monster named Chronos.[14] A poem of Alkman may name Thetis as the first divinity to exist.[15] Romm notes that the primordial water that precedes an ordered universe in Near Eastern cosmologies may be analogous to the giants that are eliminated in the ordering of the Greek cosmos.[16] All of this evidence suggests a widespread belief in the originative power of water, whether origins are understood in terms of mythology or natural philosophy.

Plato, looking back on the mythological and philosophical cosmologies, reconciles these approaches in a way that involves Okeanos as an originative force. In the *Theaetetus*, he describes Okeanos as a poetic metaphor for Heraclitus's theory of flux (152e). Aristotle, too, embraced the identification, linking

---

11. Heidel 1951, 79.
12. Translation by Heidel 1951, 72.
13. Parallels also exist with the Old Testament, particularly the emergence of the universe from a watery chaos (Heidel 1951, 82).
14. Rudhardt 1971, 13-14.
15. West 1963, 154-55. Slatkin (1991, 82-83) notes that the ancient commentary through which we know Alkman's poem interpreted the text as a cosmogony that designated Thetis as the first entity to emerge from undifferentiated matter at the beginning of the universe. See below on the connection of Thetis's name with the verb τίθημι.
16. Romm 1992, 24.

Okeanos to the theory of Thales rather than Heraclitus.[17] Indeed, the intellectual primacy of Homer later motivated extended allegorizations of the *Iliad* and *Odyssey*, in which the cosmological primacy of Okeanos is preserved.[18]

Clearly, Okeanos, although not the first principle in every Greek cosmogony, can be seen as filling the role of primordial water in Greek thought. The geography of Okeanos reflects an association with the beginning of the universe as well. In early Greek thought, Okeanos borders the world, neatly answering the question, "What lies beyond what we see?" This finite answer at the same time implies the infinite: as a circular river, Okeanos has no end. Likewise, as a progenitor, Okeanos contains the potential for all things. Geographically, as the outermost boundary of the world, Okeanos contains all within its limits. Okeanos also embodies the tension between similarity and difference: it represents the single origin of the varied contents of the world, as well as the idea that however much one seems to travel, sailing on the river Okeanos will eventually result in a return to the point of origin.

Even once the Greeks began to see the world's origins not in terms of anthropomorphic powers but in terms of physical processes, water remained a starting point. The presocratic philosophers, inquiring into the origin and composition of the cosmos, gave water a prominent position in their theories. Indeed, the first of the Milesian natural philosophers, Thales, named water as the essential substance of the world from which all else originated.[19] Subsequently, Anaximenes considered *aer* the generative material of the world, an idea that may not represent as much of a departure from Thales's theory as it might seem. As Kahn points out, *aer* originally meant "mist" or "vapor" and its association with evaporation and condensation may have suggested it to Anaximenes.[20] This sort of variety within a single substance must have been striking and may have suggested itself as a way of understanding and classifying the multiplicity of substances one observes in the world as a whole.

Water as a metaphor for transformation also coexists in myth and scientific thinking. Heraclitus, in particular, uses the mutability of water as a model for the universe. Kahn argues that Heraclitus's identification of fire as a basic substance

---

17. Kirk et al. 1993, 15.

18. Romm 1992, 179.

19. οἱ δ' ἐφ' ὕδατος κεῖσθαι (*sc.* φασὶ τὴν γῆν). τοῦτον γὰρ ἀρχαιότατον παρειλήφαμεν τὸν λόγον, ὅν φασιν εἰπεῖν Θαλῆν τὸν Μιλήσιον, ὡς διὰ τὸ πλωτὴν εἶναι μένουσαν ὥσπερ ξύλον ἤ τι τοιοῦτον ἕτερον (Arist. *Cael.* B13, 294a28); τῶν δὴ πρωτοφιλοσοφησάντων οἱ πλεῖστοι τὰς ἐν ὕλης εἴδει μόνας ᾠήθησαν ἀρχὰς εἶναι πάντων . . . τὸ μέντοι πλῆθος καὶ τὸ εἶδος τῆς τοιαύτης ἀρχῆς οὐ τὸ αὐτὸ πάντες λέγουσιν, ἀλλὰ Θαλῆς μὲν ὁ τῆς τοιαύτης ἀρχηγὸς φιλοσοφίας ὕδωρ εἶναι φησιν (Aristotle, *Meteorologica* A3, 983b6).

20. Kahn 1979, 19. Hippolytus (*Refutation* 1.7.1-3) spells out the transformations condensation brings about in *aer*: Ἀναξιμένης . . . ἀέρα ἄπειρον ἔφη τὴν ἀρχὴν εἶναι, ἐξ οὗ τὰ γινόμενα καὶ τὰ γεγονότα καὶ τὰ ἐσόμενα καὶ θεοὺς καὶ θεῖα γίνεσθαι, τὰ δὲ λοιπὰ ἐκ τῶν τούτου ἀπογόνων. τὸ δὲ εἶδος τοῦ ἀέρος τοιοῦτον· ὅταν μὲν ὁμαλώτατος ᾖ, ὄψει ἄδηλον, δηλοῦσθαι δὲ τῷ ψυχρῷ καὶ τῷ θερμῷ καὶ τῷ νοτερῷ καὶ τῷ κινουμένῳ. κινεῖσθαι δὲ ἀεί· οὐ γὰρ μεταβάλλειν ὅσα μεταβάλλει, εἰ μὴ κινοῖτο. πυκνούμενον γὰρ καὶ ἀραιούμενον διάφορον φαίνεσθαι· ὅταν γὰρ εἰς τὸ ἀραιότερον διαχυθῇ, πῦρ γίνεσθαι, ἀνέμους δὲ πάλιν πίλησιν, ἔτι δὲ μᾶλλον ὕδωρ, ἐπὶ πλεῖον πυκνωθέντα γῆν καὶ εἰς τὸ μάλιστα πυκνότατον λίθους.

stems not from a physical theory, in which other materials are derived from fire, but from the idea that fire encompasses both destruction and vitality, evanescence and constancy.[21] This interest in process rather than substance characterizes Heraclitus's statements about water as well. For him, the river is an analogy for the cosmos. The river represents something of which the whole stays the same while its constituent parts continually change. The fragments express this idea in several forms, only one of which, according to Kahn, is unmistakably Heraclitean in style.[22] This fragment, which does not go beyond a statement of fact to reveal the implications of that fact, has received a number of interpretations:

> ποταμοῖσι τοῖσιν αὐτοῖσιν ἐμβαίνουσιν ἕτερα καὶ ἕτερα ὕδατα ἐπιρρεῖ
> (Heraclitus, *Fragment* 12, Arius Didymus *ap.* Eusebium, *Praeparatio Evangelica* XV, 20)

> Upon those (same men?) who step into the same rivers, different and different waters flow.

The short statement is filled with complexity and (possibly intentional) ambiguity. Are the men or the rivers the same? Or both? Does Heraclitus mean to emphasize the sameness of the rivers or the difference of their waters? What does this analogy reveal about his theories? Kahn suggests that the emphasis should be on the continuity underlying the constant change that occurs in a river.[23] This tension between sameness and difference comes through stylistically as well. As Kahn notes, the ambiguity of αὐτοῖσιν could be eliminated if Heraclitus referred to either men or rivers in the singular.[24] As Heraclitus wrote it, however, the very word meaning "same" creates two different interpretations.[25] The repeated ἕτερα in the second half of the sentence provides a contrast: there, Heraclitus repeats a word that in each instance refers to ὕδατα. The repetition evokes change that continues over time and also may suggest that αὐτοῖσιν refers to both rivers and men. Kahn argues that the first half of the sentence better illuminates Heraclitus's thought than does the second, that is, Heraclitus emphasizes that a river (or a person, if αὐτοῖσιν refers to the men as well) can remain the same even given constant change because it has an identity that goes beyond the particular matter that forms it.[26]

---

21. Kahn 1979, 23; κόσμον τόνδε οὔτε τις θεῶν οὔτε ἀθρώπων ἐποίησεν, ἀλλ᾽ ἦν ἀεὶ καὶ ἔστιν καὶ ἔσται· πῦρ ἀείζωον, ἁπτόμενον μέτρα καὶ ἀποσβεννύμενον μέτρα (Clement, *Stromateis* 5.104.1).

22. Kahn 1979, 167.

23. Kahn 1979, 168. This also is the view of Reinhardt (1985, 177, 206f.) and Burnet (1957, 145-47).

24. Kahn 1979, 167.

25. Heraclitus's interest in human nature is otherwise attested as well. Diodotus, writing in the Hellenistic period, claims that Heraclitus's book was more about life in society than about the nature of the universe (Diels 1901, vii). See below on the river as a way of envisioning one particular type of development in a society, namely colonization.

26. Kahn 1979, 168.

Plato and Aristotle, however, stress the idea of change implied in Heraclitus's statement even though the original emphasis seems to have been placed on the continuity a river implies. Plato's expression, πάντα ῥεῖ (*Cratylus* 439C-D), seems ultimately to have become the lens through which later writers saw Heraclitus.[27] Aristotle goes beyond Plato to connect Heraclitus's idea with imperceptible changes.[28] Although it seems unlikely that Heraclitus intended this interpretation, given his insistence on the evidence of the senses,[29] rivers themselves may lead to this conclusion. Rivers, particularly in Greece, are notoriously changeable, alternately flooding and drying up altogether. The river provides the perfect metaphor for change as it often appears in nature: ever-present, often cyclical and balanced, yet not always observable in the short term or on a large scale.

In fact, Heraclitus's focus on the continuity of rivers may have been the more revolutionary idea, given the essential character of rivers in Greek myth. There, change is one of the primary identifying features of rivers as they are conceived of as gods. The earliest descriptions of shape-shifting, however, apply the property to marine deities. Proteus metamorphoses in the *Odyssey* (4.385ff.) and Heraclitus sees this mythical figure as an allegory for the initial substance from which the universe was created.[30] Thetis changes shape to escape the wooing of Peleus in Pindar's *Nemean* 4 (101-6). In addition, the mortal Mestra gets her shape-changing ability as a gift from Poseidon.[31] Forbes Irving notes the coincidence between shape-shifting ability and marine deities, but denies that their tendency to alter their form reflects "the natural fluidity of water."[32] Claiming that ancient authors do not focus on water's ability to assume various forms, Forbes Irving connects the shape-shifters' talent with their status as marginal figures, women, or old men.[33] The liminality of these figures, however, is not entirely independent of their association with water. Rather, we see a constellation of qualities that connect these characters with problematized boundaries. An identity as a marginal figure, the ability to shape-shift, and a connection with water, a substance known for its versatility, all reinforce the appropriateness of these characters as symbols of change and instability. In addition, water as a geographical feature necessarily has a defined edge and, particularly in the form of rivers, often marks a boundary. Islands have a similar significance, as they represent a liminal state and mediate between land and sea, as Borca has

---

27. λέγει που ῾Ηράκλειτος ὅτι πάντα χωρεῖ καὶ οὐδὲν μένει, καὶ ποταμοῦ ῥοῇ ἀπεικάζων τὰ ὄντα λέγει ὡς δὶς ἐς τὸν αὐτὸν ποταμὸν οὐκ ἂν ἐμβαίης (Plato, *Cratylus* 402A). This understanding of Heraclitus will appear in Ovid's *Metamorphoses*, where, in addition to representing the popular understanding of Heraclitus, the sentiment suits Ovid's theme admirably (see below).

28. καί φασί τινες κινεῖσθαι τῶν ὄντων οὐ τὰ μὲν τὰ δ᾽ οὔ, ἀλλὰ πάντα καὶ ἀεί, ἀλλὰ λανθάνειν τοῦτο τὴν ἡμετέραν αἴσθησιν (Aristotle, *Physics* Θ3, 253b9).

29. Kirk et al. 1993, 195.

30. Heraclitus, *Allegories* 64-67. See Rudhardt 1971, 21-24.

31. Fantham 1993, 25.

32. Forbes Irving 1990, 173.

33. Forbes Irving 1990, 179.

demonstrated.[34] These tendencies in myth reinforce the rationalizing theories in which water was seen as an analogy for the idea of change.

Detienne and Vernant follow this line of thinking, as they connect the propensity of sea deities for self-transformation with the gods' status as beginning points for creation: their originative nature enables them to take on any shape.[35] Indeed, Thetis's name may have cosmological significance through a connection with τίθημι. A name derived from the term used to signify founding or establishing would be especially fitting for a divinity involved in the early stages of the cosmos, as Thetis seems to have been, given her familial relationship to Nereus, the shape-shifting Old Man of the Sea.[36] This connection between presence at the beginning of creation and continued mutability may have influenced presocratic cosmogonies, which make water a basic substance as well as a model for change in the universe as a whole.

It is difficult to say at what point shape-changing attached itself to river gods. The closest Homer comes to a shape-shifting river god is the Skamander. The poet compares this river to a bull, based on the sound it makes as it ejects bodies of fallen soldiers from its stream:

> τοὺς ἔκβαλλε θύραζε, μεμυκὼς ἠΰτε ταῦρος,
> χέρσονδε· ζωοὺς δὲ σάω κατὰ καλὰ ῥέεθρα,
> κρύπτων ἐν δίνῃσι βαθείῃσιν μεγάλῃσι.
>
> (Homer, *Iliad* 21.237-39)

He casts them [sc. the dead] out onto dry land, bellowing like a bull; but the living he saves beneath the lovely stream, hiding them in great deep eddies.

The context—Achilles's battle with the Skamander—perhaps lends itself to imagining the river god's appearance, since it is left to the reader's imagination whether Achilles simply struggles with dangerous currents or actually engages in combat with a god. Interestingly, the suggestion of an animate form for the river comes at the point when it seems that the Skamander engages in rational thought: the river distinguishes between the living and the dead when expelling combatants from or covering them with the stream. In this way, the Skamander enacts one of the essential functions of a river: that of boundary. The river's actions anthropomorphize the liminal nature of a river, particularly the Styx. As the Skamander differentiates and separates the living from the dead, it represents the role of a river as a point of transition between one place and another or one state and another.

Whether Homer's simile is a precursor of the identification of river gods with bulls or a rationalizing reflection of such a belief remains unclear, but it seems possible that lost epics detailing the Herakles myth might have included the struggle between this character and the shape-shifting Achelous, an episode

---

34. Borca 2000, 203.
35. Detienne and Vernant 1978, 143.
36. Detienne and Vernant 1978, 141, paraphrasing a scholium to Lycophron.

familiar from Sophocles's *Trachiniae*. In that play, Herakles fights a bull-shaped Achelous (*Trachiniae* 509). At the beginning of the play, Deianeira mentions serpentine and part-man, part-bull as other possible shapes. It is possible that the association of bulls with Poseidon contributes to their identification with water gods.[37] Indeed, there may not have been a sharp distinction between marine and riverine deities. Rather, shape-shifting may have been a property shared by both groups. Farnell proposes that Poseidon began his existence as a freshwater god who came to be associated with the sea after his adoption by seafaring Greeks.[38] This overlap may find a parallel in the identification of Okeanos both with a body of salt water clearly different from freshwater lakes, rivers, and springs as well as with a river that encircles the earth and plays a generative role in the formation of the world.[39]

Much of river gods' shape-shifting is done for the purpose of evading capture. The difficulty of restraining these divinities mirrors the unpredictability of rivers and the ease with which water can flow away and be lost. The rewards for capturing a shape-shifter also mirror those for taming a river: one who harnesses god or water receives resources, whether they be a cornucopia from Achelous, knowledge from Proteus, or the fertile land that results from a well-regulated water supply.

Ovid's *Metamorphoses* seems a natural place to look for the association of rivers with changes in shape. Indeed, we find that Ovid's river gods frequently bring about transformations. In addition, physical contact with water can stimulate changes. These two ways in which water causes metamorphosis exemplify the two approaches to change found in Ovid's poem. A work that relies heavily on myths of transformation is framed by a philosophical cosmogony in book 1 and a speech of Pythagoras in book 15 that appeals to scientific theories for an explanation of change. In this way, the poem itself suggests two analytical frameworks that may apply, perhaps hinting at transformations that can occur even in the mind's understanding of natural phenomena.[40]

Despite the common subject matter in these two views of the universe, their proponents, the poet and Pythagoras, repeatedly emphasize the incompatibility

---

37. Farnell 1896, vol. iv 22, 26.

38. Farnell 1896, vol. iv 6. Farnell points to the etymology of Poseidon's name as an indication that he was connected with rivers (1896, vol. iv 22, 26). Pindar (*Olympian* 6.58) and Aeschylus (*Seven Against Thebes* 309) testify to Poseidon's connection with rivers as well as with the sea. Another possible connection is with Demeter. Powell interprets the name as "husband of Demeter" (2001, 152). This pairing perhaps suggests earth and water as essential forces.

39. The location of Okeanos at the rim of Achilles's shield in the *Iliad* (18.607) indicates that a concrete idea of the river's location existed, as does the belief that the stars set in Okeanos (*Iliad* 18.489). Explorations outside the straits of Gibraltar, however, revealed a saltwater ocean rather than a river. Although some poets attempted to resolve this contradiction by positing that Okeanos lay beyond this ocean (OCD s.v. Oceanus), there seems to have been some identification of Okeanos with the ocean observed outside the Mediterranean (Hecataeus, as summarized by Herodotus 4.8). Like the Skamander in *Iliad* 21, here Okeanos acts as a border, demarcating the earth as well as containing the ecphrastic description of the shield.

40. Colebrook 1997, 200.

of their approaches. Each comments on the other's material in terms of disbelief. Ovid introduces Pythagoras with what amounts to a disclaimer:

> primusque animalia mensis
> arguit inponi, primus quoque talibus ora
> docta quidem solvit, sed non et credita, verbis.
>
> (Ovid, *Metamorphoses* 15.72-74)[41]

He first disapproved of animals being put on tables, he also first opened his learned mouth with words of the following sort, but they were not believed.

Pythagoras, in turn, expresses his own disbelief in material like that found in the first fourteen books:

> esse viros fama est in Hyperborea Pallene,
> qui soleant levibus velari corpora plumis,
> cum Tritoniacam noviens subiere paludem;
> haut equidem credo: sparsae quoque membra venenis
> exercere artes Scythides memorantur easdem.
>
> (Ovid, *Metamorphoses* 15.356-60)

There is a tale that there are men in Hyperborean Pallene, who are accustomed to clothe their bodies with light feathers, when they have submerged themselves nine times in the Tritonian marsh; indeed I do not believe it: the Scythian women also are said to employ the same arts when they have sprinkled their limbs with potions.

Whereas Pythagoras's didactic mode often leads him to encourage readers with such phrases as *docebo* (15.238), *nonne vides* (15.361), and *cernimus* (15.421), here he immediately distances himself from the information with *fama est*. It seems that this mythological material lies outside Pythagoras's expertise. Thus, he can offer the tale only on the authority of another. Indeed, this brief tale resembles Ovid's aitiological metamorphoses in the first fourteen Books. *Haut equidem credo* further dissociates Pythagoras from the information he has presented, but attributed to another. Now he not only is unable to vouch for the story, but also doubts it.[42]

The vexed relationship between these two voices, of the poet and Pythagoras, has attracted significant scholarly attention.[43] I hope to show that the

---

41. Galinsky (1998, 321) interprets this statement as applying to the whole speech, not just the portion on vegetarianism. Ovid applies this rhetoric to himself in his later characterization of the *Metamorphoses* in *Tristia* 2.63-64:

inspice maius opus, quod adhuc sine fine tenetur,

   in non credendos corpora versa modos.

Behold a greater work, which is still incomplete: bodies turned into incredible forms.

42. Cf. Pythagoras's reaction to an *aition* involving centaurs: *nisi vatibus omnis eripienda fides* (*Metamorphoses* 15.282-83).

43. Fränkel believes Ovid intended the speech of Pythagoras to "provide the theoretical background for the epic of transformations" but did not succeed: "the accord between the doctrine as

differences between the approach taken in the mythological material and that of the philosophical speech of Pythagoras only emphasize the universality of metamorphosis as a concept. As Otis asserts, the philosophical content is not a way of explaining or rationalizing the myths, but stands on equal footing with the mythological *aitia* and provides an alternative explanation of some of the same phenomena the myths treat. A close look at the structure of the opening of the *Metamorphoses* and the speech of Pythagoras as well as an examination of the role water plays in each will support this idea. The speech also serves as a preparation for the Augustan material that neither endorses nor undercuts that material. Rather, Pythagoras's speech brings the subject of metamorphosis into the realm of popular science (as Galinsky notes), a necessary step in integrating a contemporary metamorphosis (Caesar's) with more ancient myths.

First, let us examine the way in which poet and philosopher begin their accounts. In *Metamorphoses* 1, Ovid, after introducing his poem, begins with a cosmogony involving divine powers that order the universe by separating out land, sky, sea, and the heavens (1.21-25). As becomes clear from the following lines, these parts of the cosmos represent fire, air, earth, and water (1.26-31). After describing the composition of the universe and the creation of living creatures (1.32-88), the poet recounts the ages, from gold to iron (1.89-150). Pythagoras, after introducing his theory of reincarnation, describes the universe in terms of the four elements (15.237-51), citing their ability to change into one another as evidence of the essential nature of change. He goes on to offer the transition from golden to iron age as additional evidence for continual change in the cosmos (15.259-61).

Although the poet and Pythagoras differ in that divine will directs the cosmos in one account and physical mechanisms in the other, the outward appearances of the universes they describe are similar. Another case in which two explanations are governed by common principles is the case for continuity despite change. Pythagoras claims the soul that undergoes reincarnation is like wax that

---

expounded here and the substance of the entire work is only superficial" (1945, 110). Otis suggests that the poet "saw the wider implications of change and was ready to treat philosophy and mythology as more or less convertible explanations of nature" but that this "does not imply anything more than that he was a reasonably educated man of his time" (1966, 394). As to its function, Otis claims that the speech "atone[s]" for the anti-Augustan aspects of the *Metamorphoses* (1966, 336). Segal takes issue with this latter point, asserting that the last books of the *Metamorphoses* "may in fact be far closer to the light and irreverent spirit of the 'true' Ovid than Otis and others have indicated" (1969, 258). He also observes that the vegetarianism Pythagoras recommends is not, in the world of the *Metamorphoses*, enough to prevent cannibalism because people become plants as well as animals (Segal 1969, 283), and this argues against the speech explaining the myths. Little recommends we not look too closely, as the relationship between myth and philosophy has only "superficial correspondence with his subject matter" (1970, 360). Knox (1986, 66, 70-74) and Hardie (1995, 204-7) argue for the literary significance of the speech: it isn't so much the philosophy as the poetic genealogy of the philosophy that counts. Galinsky argues that the natural philosophy of Pythagoras's speech is important but that it represents the popular natural philosophy at Rome, which contained a heavy dose of paradoxography. Galinsky notes that Ovid's methods in Pythagoras's speech resemble those of popular interpretations of Pythagorean philosophy, which extensively catalogue *mirabilia* (1998, 317).

retains its identity as wax even when it is stamped with different impressions (15.169-72). Ovid apparently ascribes to the same principle in crafting his mythical metamorphoses. Frequently, a vestige of an individual's identity persists through transformation into a new form. It might be tears, as in the case of Niobe (6.146-312), talent, as in the case of Arachne (6.1-145), or consciousness, as in the cases of Io (1.568-746) and Actaeon (3.138-252).

When it comes to the properties of water in metamorphoses, poet and philosopher also agree. As we have seen in this section, water is a crucial part of most ancient cosmogonies, so it is likely to be important to Ovid as an emblem of the universe's origin and development. Perhaps for this reason, water, more than any other single substance, plays an active role in metamorphosis.[44] Numerous mythical transformations involve water, often as an agent of metamorphosis. This association alone may evoke scientific beliefs about the transformative powers of water. In *Metamorphoses* 1, Daphne is changed by her river-god father, Peneus, and Syrinx by her sisters, the daughters of Ladon. In both cases, Ovid suggests that the rivers themselves had something to do with the metamorphosis:

> viribus absumptis expalluit illa citaeque
> victa labore fugae spectans Peneidas undas
> "fer, pater," inquit "opem! si flumina numen habetis,
> qua nimium placui, mutando perde figuram!"
>
> (Ovid, *Metamorphoses* 1.543-47)

Her strength gone, she grew pale and defeated by the exertion of her swift flight, catching sight of the Peneian waves, she said, "Father, bring help! If you, waters, hold divine power, destroy this shape, by which I pleased too much, by changing it!"

> hic illam cursum inpedentibus undis
> ut se mutarent liquidas orasse sorores,
>
> (Ovid, *Metamorphoses* 1.703-4)

Here, when the waves hindered her course she begged her liquid sisters that they change her.

With *flumina* and *liquidas*, Ovid balances the perception of these divinities as anthropomorphic entities with references to the physical substance they represent, perhaps implying that the transformations may be seen in terms of physical phenomena.

Pythagoras too, cites numerous instances of water acting as an agent of transformation (15.307-36, 356-60). Examples are presented in quick succession and the tone is one of objective reporting. As a character, Pythagoras artfully

---

44. This circumstance was not overlooked in a recent dramatic production (2001 at the Second Stage Theater, New York) of Ovid's *Metamorphoses*, which employed a large pool of water as the primary stage set (Zimmerman and Slavitt 2002).

recreates popular philosophy at Rome, both in terms of content and style. Galinsky notes that a variety of philosophical and scientific ideas had been included under the heading "Pythagoras" in Ovid's time.[45] In addition to philosophy, Roman popular science was influenced by the genre of paradoxography, which catalogues strange natural phenomena. These lists seem to have become canonical, given the overlap that occurs among authors. Hellenistic scholarly interest in this area of study may have made the interest in marvels part of Roman popular science. Callimachus's packaging of this sort of content as raw material for poetry (his *Hypomnemata*) may have suggested it to Roman poets.

Four of the eleven rivers and springs Pythagoras mentions also appear in the collection *Paradoxographorum Graecorum Reliquiae*.[46] The properties listed there agree with Ovid's descriptions. Such technical authors as Strabo, Vitruvius, Pausanias, and Pliny the Elder preserve additional marvels. Like the paradoxographers, they tend to describe the phenomena only briefly and tend not to speculate on the reasons for the water's unusual abilities. Pliny, in *Natural History* 2.230, gives an impressive list of rivers and springs that cause color changes, but he generally does not explain them and reports them uncritically.[47] Strabo questions the validity of some claims about water. Although he reports without passing judgment the effects of Sybaris and Crathis (*Geography* 6.1.13), he discounts the properties of Arethusa (*Geography* 6.2.4) and Salmacis (*Geography* 14.2.16).[48] Vitruvius occasionally attempts rationalizing explanations, but only of a general nature. In many of these cases, he makes an attempt at explanation but adds little information, as is the case with his statements that the properties of the soil influence the taste of water (*On Architecture* 8.3.12) and that the properties of the water entering the body influence color (*On Architecture* 8.3.14). Alternatively, he may apply a property of one component of the spring to the whole entity, as with sulfur springs that adopt the purifying capabilities of sulfur (*On Architecture* 8.3.4). The occasional incisive assessment also appears: Vitruvius attributes the ability of the Lyncestis to dissolve bladder stones to its acidity (*On Architecture* 8.3.17).[49] From these examples, it is evident that Ovid's Pythagoras follows a widely used style in his reporting of strange waters. This aspect of his characterization aligns him with scientific

---

45. Galinsky 1998, 314. Garbarino contends that this circumstance resulted from the identification of Pythagoras as the conduit for the arrival of Greek philosophy in Rome, specifically via contact between Pythagoras and Numa Pompilius (1973, 1-2). Ferrero cites Cicero's *Somnium Scipionis* and *De Natura Deorum* as two texts in which this sort of conflation occurs (1955, 27-29).

46. See Giannini 1966. The rivers and springs in common with Ovid are the stream of Ammon, the springs of Crathis and Sybaris, and the Lyncestian river.

47. The only explanation Pliny attempts is connecting the acidity of the Lyncestis with its ability to produce a state akin to drunkenness (*Lyncestis aqua quae vocatur acidula vini modo temulentos facit; Natural History* 2.230).

48. In the case of Arethusa, Strabo presents a well-reasoned argument refuting the idea that a river can flow through the sea without fresh and salt water mixing. On Salmacis, see below.

49. Vitruvius offers a much more convincing explication of the acidic water of the Lyncestis than Pliny does. In addition to connecting a property of the water with an observed effect, Vitruvius cites other instances of acids causing disintegration (*On Architecture* 8.3.18).

writers and places him as much in the context of contemporary investigation of phenomena as of presocratic philosophy.

The influence of paradoxography does not distinguish Pythagoras from the poet however. We can see its influence in the mythological portions of the poem, just as we can find myths in Pythagoras's speech, although there is little overlap in specific content. One of the few items treated by both the poet and Pythagoras is Salmacis. Pythagoras's description does nothing to recall its earlier discussion (*Metamorphoses* 4.285-388). Pythagoras describes drinking as the mechanism by which Salmacis has its effects on the body, whereas Ovid's other version cites bathing in the spring. The philosopher makes no mention of emasculation, Salmacis's claim to fame in its mythological incarnation. Rather, Salmacis, along with the Ethiopian lakes produces madness or lethargy. A spring that occasioned extended treatment from the poet receives from Pythagoras only a brief mention and no reference to the origin of its power. The nearly exclusive treatment of phenomena by either poet or philosopher may call attention to the fact that, despite an apparent tension between two voices, the poem in fact is the product of a single artistic vision.

The mythological description of Salmacis offers the detailed treatment one expects for a phenomenon so well suited to the theme of metamorphosis.[50] Like other water nymphs and river gods, Salmacis is at once personification and element:

> pugnantemque tenet, luctantiaque oscula carpit,
> subiectatque manus, invitaque pectora tangit,
> et nunc hac iuveni, nunc circumfunditur illac;
>
> (Ovid, *Metamorphoses* 4.358-60)

and she holds him fighting, and seizes struggling kisses, and lays hands on him, and touches his unwilling chest, and envelops the youth now on this side, now on that.

---

50. In fact, Salmacis was a popular subject of inquiry. Both Strabo and Vitruvius deny the power of the spring, giving anthropological, rather than naturalistic, explanations for the connection between this water and effeminacy. Strabo simply asserts that effeminacy is caused not by water but by wealth and immoderate living (τρυφῆς δ᾽ αἴτια οὐ ταῦτα, ἀλλὰ πλοῦτος καὶ ἡ περὶ τὰς διαίτας ἀκολασία, *Geography* 14.2.16). Martial may reflect this analysis when he relocates Salmacis and its enervating effects to the Bay of Naples, an area connected with the luxurious lifestyle (*Epigrams* 10.30.8-10). Vitruvius offers a more detailed scenario, specific to the location but still focused on customs rather than chemistry. He links the belief to a specific event, explaining that an inn run by Greek colonists near this salubrious water attracted barbarians and thus introduced them to civilization (*On Architecture* 2.8.12). In a way, Strabo and Vitruvius have constructed their own "mythology" of Salmacis, making the story seem more plausible while at the same time adapting it to their own ends: the architect sees the virtues of civilization and the Stoic decries luxury. There is an inscription from Halicarnassus that joins praise of Salmacis with an account of Greek colonization of Halicarnassus. The myth prefigures the colonization by detailing the means by which a newly arrived individual (Hermaphroditus) becomes forever bound to his new home (Isager 1998, 14). See below on colonization. See also Lloyd-Jones 1999, 1-14; Lloyd-Jones 1999a, 63-65; Austin 1999, 92.

As encoded in the verbs, Salmacis's behavior is at once appropriate to a human form (*subiectat, tangit*) and to water (*circumfunditur*). Hermaphroditus's prayer, however, makes explicit the idea that the water itself will take on transformative powers independent of the supernatural abilities of the nymph:

> "nato date munera vestro,
> et pater et genetrix, amborum, nomen habenti:
> quisquis in hos fontes vir venerit, exeat inde
> semivir et tactis subito mollescat in undis!"
> motus uterque parens nati rata verba biformis
> fecit et incesto fontem medicamine tinxit.

(Ovid, Metamorphoses 4.383-88)

"Grant these favors, mother and father, to your son who has the name of both: whatever man comes into this spring, may he go out from it half a man and may he grow soft at once as he touches the water!" Each parent, moved, accomplished the words of the two-formed son and tinged the spring with an impure potion.

The *aition* transfers the power of change from nymph to water. The water does not gain its permanent power simply by divine edict, however. There is a chemical explanation for the water's new property. Hermes and Aphrodite add a potion (*medicamine*, 388), which will enable the spring to have its effect on future swimmers without subsequent divine involvement. Salmacis has been effectively transferred from the realm of myth to the realm of natural phenomenon.

Likewise in the myth of Actaeon, divine will combines with physical properties. Actaeon grows horns after Diana sprinkles his head with water (*Metamorphoses* 3.189-90, 193-94). Although Actaeon's whole body changes to that of a stag, the metamorphosis begins with his head, where the water touched him, suggesting that, in addition to the goddess's will, contact with the water is responsible for turning man to deer. Two of the apotheoses in the *Metamorphoses* also have this combination of divine intervention and water as a means of change. In books 13 and 14, gods use river water to remove the mortal nature from Glaucus and Aeneas. Okeanos and Tethys repeat an incantation nine times and then have Glaucus bathe in one hundred rivers to render him immortal (*Metamophoses* 13.951-55). Just one river, the Numicus, is required to make Aeneas immortal. Again, Ovid envisions the process as one of washing (*Metamorphoses* 14.600-604). These episodes reflect the custom of washing the dead in fresh water and suggest that the act has significance beyond cleansing the body and represents the transition to a new state of being.[51]

Pythagoras employs alternative explanations and, indeed, offers a very similar *aition*, for the spring that follows Salmacis in his list, Clitor (Ovid, *Metamorphoses* 15.322-28): either that the water itself has some power or that Melampus doctored the water with herbs that promote lucidity. From these ex-

---

51. See below, ch. 2.

amples we see that the same methodology of explanation can exist in both poetic and philosophical contexts, a circumstance that contradicts the ostensible disagreement of Ovid's two voices. By placing the account of Clitor immediately after Pythagoras's description of Salmacis, Ovid undercuts any conflict that the differing reports on Salmacis might imply.

Specific, preexisting properties of the water of a particular river or spring often have something to do with the nature of the transformation that takes place. Io is changed back into human form at the Nile, a river famous for its ability to generate life (Ovid, *Metamorphoses* 1.738-46). The Nile also is notable for its location in Egypt, a land that Herodotus described as being in every way the opposite of Greece.[52] As such, this river is the perfect place for a reversal. The motionless pool beside which Narcissus sits perfectly reflects his stillness and suits equally well the plant that he becomes (*Metamorphoses* 3.406-36). The power of water is more latent in these examples than in those cited previously, but its properties help account for the transformations occurring in its environment.

As the above examples demonstrate, the behavior of water in metamorphosis follows a set of rules common to the mythological and philosophical portrayals of transformation. We can conclude that for Ovid, whether he uses the voice of the poet or, for example, of Pythagoras, one aspect of the power of water is its role in generating the universe, contact with water is one way to stimulate metamorphosis, a particular type of water may motivate a transformation that is in keeping with the properties of that water, and the paradoxographical tradition is a likely source for style and content in descriptions of particular bodies of water. Thus, poet and philosopher are operating under the same assumptions about water as a substance (and, indeed, both adhere to the Greco-Roman cultural understanding of water) and seem to have common sources for their information. It seems, therefore, that the poet and Pythagoras have more in common than their protestations would indicate. While ostensibly presenting two different views of the universe, Ovid in fact emphasizes the constant properties of the universe. The change, in fact, occurs at the level of interpretation rather than observation.

Ovid's poem, by taking change as its subject, continually highlights that change against a backdrop of continuity. This approach mirrors the perpetual scientific quest to discern a small number of essential substances or principles that explains the infinite variety of the observable world. The ideas of origin and transformation are, thus, inextricably linked in envisioning the development of the cosmos. In the preceding section, we have examined a number of contexts in which water plays a crucial role in understanding that process of development. The ubiquity of water in cosmogonies suggests that, for Mediterranean and Near Eastern societies, this familiar substance provides the best analogy between human life and the history of the universe.

---

52. Herodotus, *History* 2.35-36.

Chapter Two

Ritual

The ritual role of water also depends on its association with change, although in ritual we are more often concerned with metaphysical change than with physical transformation. In a ritual context, water frequently marks a transition from one state to another without any outwardly visible change.[1] As with cosmologies, temporality comes into play when we consider the ritual role of water. Most rituals involving water concern transitions from one phase of life to another.

River water plays a role in a number of ritual observances in the ancient world, particularly purifications.[2] While salt water may also be a purifying substance,[3] fresh water is more commonly associated with several important rites of passage. At coming of age ceremonies, Greek youths dedicated locks of hair to a local river god. Before marriage, bride and groom bathe. Finally, water is important in funerary ritual, both for washing the corpse and for cleansing the mourners.

All of these rituals mark a transition as well as establishing or acknowledging a connection with a god or gods. We see the connection between these ideas clearly in ancient beliefs about crossing rivers. Hesiod cautions that one should never cross a river without praying and washing one's hands in the stream (*Works and Days* 737-41). In performing this small ritual, one who crosses a boundary first establishes contact with the presiding divinity through both physical and psychological means. Prayer acknowledges the divine nature of the presiding entity and the washing of hands signals an understanding that the power is linked to a physical substance, from which it is inseparable. The con-

---

1. Washing was the first step in funerary ritual and served a practical purpose (cleansing the body of blood or other stains in order to prevent contagion), but also had a ceremonial function analogous to the role of water in other rites of passage such as birth and marriage (Vermeule 1979, 13).

2. "Among agents of purification, the most widely used and most basic was water. . . . Lustral water had to be pure, and drawn from a flowing source; so too, if possible, water for ordinary washing. But no washerwoman would think of combining the waters of three, five, seven, or fourteen different springs to remove even the deepest stain. . . . Particular springs were especially favoured for purifications, and the most prized cathartic water was that of the salt-stained sea." (Parker 1996, 226).

3. Parker 1996, 226-27.

nection is made equally in thought and action and the river is acknowledged as both substance and god. We see the same principle at work in the Roman Forum, in the guise of the god Janus, who was worshipped at crossing points of the Forum brook. These crossings were inaugurated with shrines to Janus in order to obviate the need for repetitive performances of the river crossing ritual.[4] The title of Rome's chief priest bears witness to the importance of water crossings as well. The term *pontifex* derives from *pons* and denotes a bridgemaker. Hallett argues that the oldest bridge over the Tiber, the *pons sublicius*, was designed to provide a safe crossing in the ritual as well as in the practical sense. The *pontifex*, then, comes to preside over the safety of the community in a more general context as well.[5]

In the less literal river crossings of life, contact with the gods also is made through contact with water. One crossing that blends physical with metaphysical is, of course, the belief that the souls of the departed must cross the river Styx on their way to the underworld. The ultimate transition of life is visualized as a familiar type of ritualized border crossing. There is a temporal element to all of these rites of passage and they are one-way trips. In this respect, they resemble a river not in its identity as a boundary, but as a directional flow of water. The river resembles time, passing in only one direction.[6] Once a rite of passage is accomplished, one's status has changed and (normally at least) there is no going back.

Having examined the links between rivers and rites of passage, let us now turn to the specifics of the rituals, particularly those surrounding funerals, since these have spawned numerous literary treatments. First, however, let us examine some rituals that occur during life. In Greek tradition, a lock of hair might be dedicated to a local river god at a coming of age ceremony.[7] River gods were recipients of these dedications probably via their role as protectors of the young.[8] As Burkert points out, this dedication signifies a rite of passage that is irrevocable, since the item left behind is never retrieved.[9] Hera and Juno, both important goddesses in the context of marriage, are associated with water, Hera at her cult sites and Juno through titles such as Fluvonia. In Greek marriage ritual, bride and groom each took a ritual bath before the ceremony. In Roman tradition, the

---

4. Holland 1961, 25. A river is considered "living water" and, thus, requires ritual attention. The supernatural protection afforded by rivers that border one's territory translates into constraints placed on crossing when streams flow within the confines of the city (Holland 1961, 21-22). Janus, as a god presiding over these transitions, can lend his power if a shrine is placed at the point of crossing, thus making repeated ritual observances unnecessary (Holland 1961, 26-27).

5. Hallett 1970, 226-27. See also Holland 1970, 332-42 on the Italic origins of the title and office of *pontifex*.

6. On the river as time, see Ovid, *Metamorphoses* 15.180-84 and *Ars Amatoria* 3.63-64.

7. Burkert 1985, 70, 175.

8. Harrison 1988, 248.

9. Burkert 1985, 70.

aquae et ignis communicatio (sharing of water and fire) was an important part of marriage ritual.[10]

Water establishes connections between the human world and that of the gods as well as between individual members of human society. The role of river and spring water in divination also may relate to the identification of water as a gift of the gods. Through contact with water, contact with the gods can be established. The oracle at Klaros contained a spring from which a priest drank in order to become inspired by the god. At Didyma, a priestess achieved an ecstatic state by wetting her feet in a sacred spring and breathing its vapors.[11] At the oracle of Trophonius, one seeking a prophecy first washes in the river Hercyna, drinks from the spring of forgetfulness and then from the spring of memory, and then enters a cavern constructed for this purpose. After lying flat on the floor, he is pulled through a narrow gap into the shrine. Pausanias (9.39.5-14) describes the process as similar to someone caught in a river's current being pulled underwater.[12] There was also hydromancy, in which water gave signs directly (Augustine, *De Civitate Dei* 7.35; Strabo, *Geography* 16.2.39; Pliny, *Natural History* 37.192).

Water not only conveyed messages from the gods, but also could effect physical changes motivated by divine intervention. Healing sanctuaries contained sources of water and bathing in these waters was an important part of the cure.[13] Surely, the salubrious and hygenic effects of water, particularly mineral water, were recognized, but in the context of the healing sanctuary, water was one of a number of ways in which the healing divinity might affect those in need of a cure. Greek sanctuaries of Asclepius contained springs and when the god was introduced in Rome, his sanctuary was placed on the Tiber Island where it was literally surrounded by water. In addition, this liminal location places the shrine in the city yet demarcated from it.

The concept that unites all of these ritual applications of water is the idea that water is a gift of the gods.[14] Water also is itself divine, when conceived in terms of the gods and nymphs that embody it. It represents not only the sky, from which it falls as rain, but also the earth, as springs well up and rivers may seem to appear from and disappear into the ground.[15] Just as water permeates the various levels of the environment, likewise it finds its way into a wide range of rituals. Essentially, contact with water represents contact with the divine.[16] In addition, the cleansing properties of water can be envisioned on a metaphorical

---

10. Treggiari 1993, 8. Ovid attests to the importance of the rite (*Fasti* 4.791-92; Treggiari 1993, 168).

11. Burkert 1985, 115.

12. Ferguson 1980, 122-23.

13. Zaidman and Pantel 1992, 129.

14. Cole 1988, 161.

15. The myth of Arethusa illustrates the ancient belief in the chthonic associations of rivers. In addition, a real river in Arcadia named "Styx" connects the observable landscape with the invisible realm of the underworld (Herodotus, *History* 6.74; Strabo, *Geography* 8.8.4; Pausanias, *Guide to Greece* 8.17.6; Pliny, *Natural History* 2.231).

16. See Holland 1961.

level and sacred water is believed to be able to effect spiritual purification, again symbolizing the intervention of a supernatural power through the agency of water.

Funerary ritual in particular enables us to identify ritual water specifically with river water. In literary contexts, a river may stand in for human mourners and fulfill the funerary requirement that a body be washed. A river washing a corpse that falls into its stream thus serves as a metaphorical expression of ritual and emphasizes the importance of washing in the context of Greco-Roman funerary rites.

In Greek and Roman society, a proper funeral involves washing the body, anointing it with oil, and dressing it in clean clothing. Vermeule describes a Greek funeral in detail, based on literary and artistic evidence.[17] We see a similar sequence of events in Vergil's description of Misenus's funeral in the *Aeneid* :

> pars calidos latices et aena undantia flammis
> expediunt, corpusque lavant frigentis et unguent.
> fit gemitus. tum membra toro defleta reponunt
> purpureasque super vestis, velamina nota,
> coniciunt.
>
> (Vergil, *Aeneid* 6.218-22)

> Some bring forth hot water and bronze cauldrons boiling on the fire, and they wash the body of the cold one and anoint it. There is weeping. Then they place the lamented limbs on a bier and heap purple garments on top, familiar clothing.

Following the washing, anointing, and dressing, the body is laid out, usually in the home, and people come to pay their respects. Parker notes another use for water at this point in the ritual: a bowl of water from a source outside the house is placed on the doorstep so that mourners may cleanse themselves of contamination as they leave the house.[18] The funeral procession and cremation or inhumation of the body usually take place at night and are followed by purification of the participants and feasting that mark a return to the concerns of the living. This purification may be accomplished either by bathing or by sprinkling with water and also receives mention in the description of the rites for Misenus:

> idem ter socios pura circumtulit unda
> spargens rore levi et ramo felicis olivae,
> lustravitque viros dixitque novissima verba.
>
> (Vergil, *Aeneid* 6.229-31)

> He circled his comrades three times with pure water, sprinkling them with light dew and a branch of fruitful olive, and he purified the men and said final words.

---

17. Vermeule 1979, 11-23.
18. Parker 1996, 35.

Vergil describes the water used for this ritual as *pura . . . unda* (*Aenied* 6.229), a phrase that seems to indicate river water. Although *unda* often denotes sea water, it frequently refers to the current of a river. *Pura* reinforces the association with rivers, since it indicates purity not only from any additional ingredients but also from pollution in a ritual sense. River water fulfills both of these conditions and, indeed, lustral water was supposed to come from a flowing source.[19]

After the funeral, offerings continued to be made to the dead, in the form of libations. In the Greek world, *lekythoi*, the vessels from which these libations were poured, often served as grave markers and were decorated with funerary images. A design that occurs on a number of these vessels, Charon in his boat, refers to the water of the underworld.[20] For the souls themselves, water is an important part of their entry into the afterlife. Most important is the river Styx, which constitutes the boundary between this world and the next. In addition to a river crossing, river and spring water figures in other aspects of existence in the underworld. The dead must become forgetful of their lives: this is accomplished by drinking from the river Lethe. Orphic texts inscribed on gold leaves emphasize the importance of drinking from the correct spring upon arrival in the underworld.[21]

Water can cleanse the dead, but conversely, death can pollute water when a body falls into a river. Of course, the realities of battle dictate that if the dead fall into a river, the water both washes their bodies and, in turn, becomes stained with their blood. Poetic descriptions, however, exploit these facts, lending symbolic significance to topographical happenstance and physical reality. In these contexts, rivers become active participants in the scene and have a role in determining whether the deceased receives proper burial.

The ultimate source for a river participating in funerary rites in this way is *Iliad* 21, when Achilles battles in and with the Skamander. The river, for its part, attempts to defend its people against Achilles without becoming polluted or clogged with corpses:

πάντα δ᾽ ὄρινε ῥέεθρα κυκώμενος, ὦσε δὲ νεκροὺς
πολλούς, οἵ ῥα κατ᾽ αὐτὸν ἅλις ἔσαν, οὕς κτάν᾽ Ἀχιλλεύς·
τοὺς ἔκβαλλε θύραζε, μεμυκὼς ἠΰτε ταῦρος,
χέρσονδε· ζωοὺς δὲ σάω κατὰ καλὰ ῥέεθρα,
κρύπτων ἐν δίνῃσι βαθείῃσιν μεγάλῃσι.

(Homer, *Iliad* 21.235-39)

The river rose, whirling all its waters, and thrust the many dead, who were under his waves, whom Achilles killed; those he cast out, bellowing like a bull, onto dry land; but the living he saved beneath his lovely stream, hiding them in a great deep eddy.

---

19. See Parker 1996, 226. Bömer *ad* Ovid, *Fasti* 2.35 gives numerous parallels.
20. Vermeule 1979, 9.
21. Inscribed gold leaves direct souls newly arrived in the underworld to drink not from the first spring they encounter but from one further along their path (West 1975, 230).

As the river fights Achilles with raging water, it deposits slain Trojans on its banks, but hides the living beneath its waters. The introduction of fire at the end of the scene gives some insight into the river's treatment of the dead. Hephaistos sends the fire to check the Skamander, but, before reaching the river, the fire burns the corpses lying on the plain (*Iliad* 21.343-45). Although the river is not specifically described as washing the bodies, in effect that is what happens. The Skamander and Hephaistos act as a kind of metonymy for the events of a funeral. The advantage goes to the Greeks, but natural forces insure that the Trojans do not suffer the indignity of mistreatment of their dead.[22]

Ovid clearly describes a river participating in funeral rites. In *Metamorphoses* 2, the Eridanus receives Phaethon's burned body after he plummets from the chariot of the sun:

> quem procul a patria diverso maximus orbe
> excipit Eridanus fumantiaque abluit ora.
> Naiades Hesperiae trifida fumantia flamma
> corpora dant tumulo, signant quoque carmine saxum
>
> (Ovid, *Metamorphoses* 2.324-27)

> Far off from his fatherland, in a remote place, the great Eridanus catches him up and washes his smoking face. The Hesperian Naiads commit his body, smoking with the three-pronged flame, to a tomb, and they inscribe the stone with these verses . . .

Here the river washes the body, specifically Phaethon's face, while the nymphs build him a tomb.[23] This is the order in which these actions would occur in a funeral, with the washing of the corpse happening immediately after death and the preparation of the tomb following.[24] The verbs, *excipit* and *abluit*, while they can refer to the actions of water, evoke the river god as well as the physical river into which Phaethon fell.

Rivers do not necessarily participate in the burial of the enemy killed in battle, however. In Lucan's *Civil War*, Pompey expresses his distaste for battle, emphasizing universal suffering over victory and defeat:

> Quantum scelerum quantumque malorum
> in populos lux ista feret! Quot regna iacebunt!

---

22. The natural world acts in place of family members in a Serbo-Croatian folk song about a wounded warrior (Bartók and Lord 1951, 351):
Neither his mother nor his sister tend him,
Nor his newly-wed bride.
The rain washes him; the warm sun dries him.
23. In Propertius, *Elegies* 3.18, Marcellus's face is described as making contact with the Styx (*Marcellus Stygias vultum demisit in undas, / errat et inferno spiritus ile lacu* [9-10 Goold]; Marcellus has lowered his countenance into the Stygian waves, and his spirit wanders in the infernal lake).
24. Toynbee 1971, 44.

Sanguine Romano quam turbidus ibit Enipeus!

(Lucan, Civil War 7.114-16)

How much crime and how much evil this light will bring to the peoples! How many kingdoms will lie ruined! How clouded with Roman blood will the Enipeus flow!

In his third exclamation, Pompey contrasts the Roman blood with the foreign river into which it flows. The Romans impose not only their civil strife on Greece but also their blood on the Greek river. Conquerors and conquered can no longer be distinct when those fighting on both sides are Romans.[25] The river does not make a distinction either: the bodies imagined in its stream could be from either side.

In contrast to the examples we have seen of rivers that wash the dead, this river, upon which death is an unwelcome imposition, is stained with blood. Unlike the Skamander, the Enipeus in Lucan abstains from funerary rites, as evidenced by the lack of mourning and of reference to washing the bodies. The river, like a person who comes in contact with death, becomes polluted. The retained contamination perhaps suggests that death inflicted in civil war is not easily purified, even when water is abundant.

These two visions of rivers, as entities that either wash corpses or become polluted by death, figure prominently in the death of Aeneas.[26] This incident occurs outside the narrative of the *Aeneid*, but versions appear in several other authors. Livy follows the version in which Aeneas is killed battling the Etruscans at the Numicus river. Livy makes the Numicus the location for Aeneas's death, but the river does not play an active role (*Ab Urbe Condita* 1.2.6). Although he records Indiges as the name Aeneas received after his death, Livy does not personally endorse that part of the tradition. Tibullus, however, makes the river a participant by specifying that it was the waves of the Numicus that sent Aeneas to the sky (*Elegies* 2.5.39-44). Ovid goes even further and defines the mechanism by which the river confers divinity: In *Metamorphoses* 14, the Numicus, at Venus's bidding, washes away the mortal part of Aeneas:

hunc iubet Aeneae, quaecumque obnoxia morti,
abluere et tacito deferre sub aequora cursu;
corniger exsequitur Veneris mandata suisque,
quicquid in Aenea fuerat mortale, repurgat
et respersit aquis; pars optima restituit illi.
lustratum genetrix divino corpus odore
unxit et ambrosia cum dulci nectare mixta
contigit os fecitque deum, quem turba Quirini

---

25. Likewise, Lucan describes Sulla's victims as clogging the Tiber (*Civil War* 2.209ff). Just as civil killing defiles the landscape, the bodies are not cleansed by the river.

26. Both also are present also in other contexts in the *Aeneid*: Italian rivers become bloodied, and the Tiber symbolically returns Turnus to life.

nuncupat Indigetem temploque arisque recepit.

(Ovid, *Metamorphoses* 14.600-608)

> She (Venus) ordered him (the Numicus) to wash away from Aeneas whatever
> was subject to death, and to carry it under the depths with his silent course. The
> horned god[27] carried out Venus's command and with his waters cleansed and
> washed whatever had been mortal in Aeneas; the best part remained with him.
> His mother anointed with divine perfume his body, which had been washed,
> and she touched his lips with ambrosia mixed with sweet nectar and made him
> a god, whom the people of Quirinus called Indiges and received him with a
> temple and altars.

The process is similar to the funeral the Eridanus and the nymphs give Phaethon,
involving both a river and a female divinity. In this case, however, Venus, instead of making a tomb for her son, directs the river's washing of Aeneas and
then continues the ritual by anointing his body, the step that usually follows
washing. The funereal washing cleanses Aeneas of his mortal aspect. The process by which apotheosis is accomplished often involves fire.[28] Just as water can
replace fire in apocalyptic visions, so it may accomplish apotheosis in a manner
analogous to that of fire, by coming into contact with the individual to be dei-
fied. In a way, rivers are ideal agents for bringing about apotheosis: they are
gods, and thus are capable of transforming others into immortals, and, in addition, they are composed of water, an essential component of rites of transition in
the ancient world.

The material in Ovid's *Metamorphoses* that relates to the Aeneas legend
often is referred to as Ovid's reading of the *Aeneid* and, indeed, we can see hints
of the scenario Ovid describes for Aeneas's apotheosis in the *Aeneid* itself.
Likewise, a "Thirteenth Book of the *Aeneid*" written in the fifteenth century by
the Italian Mapheus Vegius is an attempt to extrapolate the events of the *Aeneid*
to their logical conclusion. The only one of a number of such sequels to become
famous, Vegius's poem was an attempt to make the form of the *Aeneid* correspond to what he saw as its true meaning: for him the epic was an allegory of the
soul.[29] Thus, the poem, wherever it began, should end, like accounts of saints'
lives, with attainment of the heavenly goal.[30] While it is clear from his hexame-
ters that Vegius was an avid reader of the *Aeneid*, he, of course, had Ovid to rely
on as well and, indeed, follows Ovid closely in his description of Aeneas's death
and translation to heaven. We should look at his description, however, because it

---

27. On river gods' horns, see ch. 3.

28. Cf. Hercules's apotheosis accomplished by fire.

29. Brinton 1930, 2. Other allegorical readings from Late Antiquity liken the journey of
Aeneas to a human life, with parts of the poem representing childhood, adolescence, and adulthood.
Fulgentius, who in the late fifth or early sixth century wrote what Baswell refers to as "the earliest
surviving systematic allegorization of the *Aeneid*," connects books of the *Aeneid* with stages of
human life: book 1 represents infancy; books 2 and 3, youth; book 4, adolescence; book 5, a return
to the values of his father; and book 6, learning; while books 7-12 receive less detailed analysis
(Baswell 1995, 96-97; Whitbread 1971, 125-35).

30. Brinton 1930, 26.

contains an important difference in the role of the Numicus. Vegius minimizes the part played by the river in washing Aeneas's body:

> Tum Venus aerias descendit lapsa per auras,
> Laurentumque petit: vicina Numicius undis
> flumineis ubi currit in aequora harundine tectus.
> tunc corpus nati abluere, et deferre sub undas
> quicquid erat mortale iubet: dehinc laeta recentem,
> felicemque animam secum super aera duxit:
> immisitque Aeneam astris, quem Iulia proles
> Indigetem appellat, templisque imponit honores.
>
> (Vegius, *Thirteenth Book of the Aeneid* 623-30)

> Then Venus descends, sliding through the light breezes, and she seeks Laurentum: near where the Numicus clothed in reeds rushes into the sea with a river's waves. Then she orders (him) to wash the body of her son, and to carry under his waves whatever was mortal: then, glad, she led the happy soul, recently freed, with her to the sky: and she sent Aeneas to the stars; the Julian line calls him Indiges, and establishes rites in temples.

While Ovid specifies that the river (*hunc*, *Metamorphoses* 14.600) performs the washing of Aeneas's body, Vegius omits the accusative, despite otherwise retaining much of Ovid's phrasing. Vegius still implies that the river does the washing, but does not make explicit reference to it. Indeed, the woodcut illustration of the scene (figure 2.1), done by Sebastian Brant for a 1502 edition of the *Aeneid* that included the thirteenth book, reflects the shift in emphasis from the river to Venus. Text and woodcut suggest that by the fifteenth and sixteenth centuries, the potency of the river as an animate part of the landscape has lapsed.

In the *Aeneid* itself, images of death in rivers refer to the death of Aeneas. We know that Vergil envisions the deification of Aeneas: in a prophecy near the end of the poem, Jupiter predicts that Aeneas will become Indiges.[31] There is no mention in that passage of the means of Aeneas's transformation, but, elsewhere in the poem, several of Vergil's references to death in rivers suggest the agency of the Numicus. Dyson discusses these and other allusions to Aeneas's death.[32] I will consider some of the passages she treats, looking specifically at the role of rivers, and, in addition, I will propose one more example. Indeed, our first view of Aeneas already prefigures his end. We first see Aeneas in a moment of despair. Buffeted by a storm off Carthage, he wishes to have died at Troy, a reasonable enough sentiment given the consequences of death at sea. One of the deaths he envisions as preferable, however, is revealing. He imagines the bodies that fell into the Simois River:

> o Danaum fortissime gentis

---

31. The etymology of the name is uncertain, but it seems to have denoted a local divinity (OLD s.v. *Indiges*).

32. Dyson 1993; Dyson 2001, 13-18.

Tydide! mene Iliacis occumbere campis
non potuisse tuaque animam hanc effundere dextra,
saevus ubi Aeacidae telo iacet Hector, ubi ingens
Sarpedon, ubi tot Simois correpta sub undis
scuta virum galeasque et fortia corpora volvit!

(Vergil, *Aeneid* 1.96-101)

O Diomedes, strongest of the Greeks, why could I not lie on Trojan fields and
why could your right hand not pour out this soul, where fierce Hector lies by
the spear of Achilles, where giant Sarpedon is, where the Simois rolls beneath
its waves the shields, helmets, and brave bodies of men that it has seized!

Figure 2.1: "Death of Aeneas" woodcut by Sebastian Brant (1502)[33]

---

33. See Brinton 1930.

Although it might seem that the *fortia corpora* in the Simois do not receive burial, the water of a native river is a better resting place for a Trojan than the sea.[34] As this passage demonstrates, Aeneas is still very much a Trojan at this point. Later in the poem we see the Simois and Xanthus transformed into the Tiber and Numicus. The transformation, however, will be far from straightforward.

Although, in her prophecy in book 6, the Sibyl equates the Tiber with the Simois and Xanthus, as an Italian river it is envisioned as hostile to the Trojans:

> bella, horrida bella,
> et Thybrim multo spumantem sanguine cerno.
> non Simois tibi nec Xanthus nec Dorica castra
> defuerint; alius Latio iam partus Achilles,
>
> (Vergil, *Aeneid* 6.86-89)

> I see wars, terrible wars, and the Tiber foaming with much blood. You will not lack a Simois or a Xanthus or a Doric camp; another Achilles has already been born in Latium . . .

This is a discouraging image for the Trojans: once again they will fight a formidable enemy beside a river, yet this time not even the topography will be familiar. They cannot expect the Tiber to behave as the Simois had.[35] The Sibyl's assurance that a Simois and Xanthus will not be lacking only serves to disquiet her listeners, since it is placed after a description of the Tiber behaving precisely as the true Simois did not (*Aeneid* 1.96-101, quoted above). The Tiber does not wash the corpses and, thus, remains bloody. The imbalance of referring to only one Italian river while mentioning two at Troy implies a companion for the Tiber. Servius remarks that Aeneas's Simois and Xanthus are "the Tiber and the Numicus, into which he fell" (*ad Aeneid* 6.88).[36] If this phrase reminds us, as it does Servius, of Aeneas's death, then the analogy may in fact imply hope for the Trojans, although at this point they are unable to understand the prediction. The implicit allusion to the Numicus may suggest that the Italian rivers will become as familiar to the Trojans as the Simois and Xanthus had been.

The Tiber, however, is not a purely partisan river. Like the Enipeus in Lucan, the Tiber objects to deaths that have the connotations of civil war. Latinus, who disapproves of the war, sees the Italian landscape as polluted by the conflict. He laments:

> bis magna victi pugna vix urbe tuemur
> spes Italas; recalent nostro Thybrina fluenta
> sanguine adhuc campique ingentes ossibus albent.
>
> (Vergil, *Aeneid* 12.34-36)

---

34. See also O'Hara 1990, 104-11.

35. There may be a reminiscence here of Achilles's battle with the Skamander, as the Simois is a tributary of the Skamander.

36. Dyson 1993, 27.

Twice conquered in great battles, we scarcely protect the Italian hopes in the
city; the Tiber's flow is still warm with our blood and huge fields are white
with bones.

Nostro juxtaposed with *Thybrina* emphasizes the pathos of Latins dying in their
own river.[37] As opposed to the Simois in *Aeneid* 1, here not only do the Tiber
and the rest of the landscape not participate in cleansing and burying the dead,
but also are made unnatural through changes in temperature and color.[38] We
must not forget, however, that this is Latinus's perception, which is colored by
his belief that war is not the answer. Nevertheless, it illustrates what seems to be
the response of a river to unwelcome bodies in its stream.

If Aeneas is to achieve his destined apotheosis in the Numicus, then, the
hostility of Italian rivers must be overcome. One way in which Vergil accomplishes this is by foreshadowing Aeneas's death in the final moments of the native Italian, Camilla. Dyson does not number Camilla among those who prefig-
ure Aeneas's death, and, indeed, she is most obviously a counterpart to Turnus:
the same line describes both of their deaths and, indeed, those deaths come
about as a result of a preoccupation with the spoils of war. For Turnus, it is the
swordbelt he took from Pallas. Aeneas sees this trophy and, in a rage, kills Turnus. Camilla's downfall is her desire for the splendid armor of a Trojan soldier.
Another Trojan, Arruns, takes advantage of her distraction and kills her. Because of the link Vergil establishes between Camilla and Turnus, Kepple contends that Arruns fulfills a role analogous to that of Aeneas.[39] The comparison is
illuminating because, while Aeneas does not die in the *Aeneid*, Arruns does.
Indeed, his death comes at the hands of Diana, as retribution for killing Camilla,
and he does not receive burial. This fate may seem appropriate for Aeneas as
well, especially given the prediction by Dido in *Aeneid* 4 that Aeneas would lie
unburied.

Rarely in the *Aeneid*, however, do one-to-one correspondences between
characters work. Consequently, there often are points of contact between a character and a number of models, both inside and outside the poem. Thus, there are
similarities between Aeneas and Arruns's foe Camilla, as well as between
Aeneas and Arruns. These multiple associations for Aeneas result in an ever
more ambiguous end not only to the poem, but also to Aeneas's life. The link

---

37. See Dyson 1993, 56ff. on the allegiance of the Tiber.
38. In *Odes* 1.2, Horace also pictures the flooding of the Tiber as unnatural and, indeed, a sign
of the gods' disfavor at Caesar's assassination. He interprets the event as a sign of divine disfavor: in
response to the destructive acts of Caesar's assassins, the city, too, will destroy itself, as indicated by
the damage done to the Regia (*Odes* 1.2.13, 20). Interpretation of flooding as a sign of divine dis-
pleasure was prevalent: a flood that blocked Otho's path as he left Rome bodes ill for his expedition
(Tacitus, *Histories* 1.86), and a flood is credited with repelling Sabine invaders early in Rome's
history (Ovid, *Fasti* 1.269-72; *Metamorphoses* 14.791-95). In fact, to make a flood a good omen
requires special pleading. When an inundation coincided with Octavian assuming the title Augustus,
Cassius Dio reports that soothsayers interpreted the event as a sign that Augustus would rise to great
heights and hold the whole city under his sway (*Roman History* 53.21). This rather contrived interpretation demonstrates the degree to which floods had negative connotations.
39. Kepple 1976, 344-60.

between Aeneas and Camilla, as we shall see, calls into question the assumption that Aeneas will reenact Arruns's death with his own. Although Arruns, dying, seems to fulfill Dido's prophecy, he is said to lie unburied on the dust (*pulvere*, *Aeneid* 11.866) rather than on sand (*harena*) as Dido had predicted (*Aeneid* 4.620). The language that describes Camilla's death, however, calls to mind the death predicted for Aeneas in earlier legend. Perhaps this is a hint: Camilla's death recalls the one element missing from Arruns's demise that would complete Dido's prediction. The implication of this hint, then, is that Camilla's kinship to the land is as important to understanding Aeneas's destiny as is Arruns's killing of one whose death leads to his own demise.

There are several specific points of contact between the actions of Aeneas and Camilla in the events leading to their deaths. Before their final conflicts, Aeneas and Camilla both are described taunting their enemies and the taunts are introduced with the same phrase (*provolvens super haec inimico pectore fatur*, *Aeneid* 10.556; *traicit et super haec inimico pectore fatur*, *Aeneid* 11.685). Brutal killing by each ensues. At the end, Aeneas is compared to a torrent or whirlwind (*talia per campos edebat funera ductor / Dardanius, torrentis aquae vel turbinis atri / more furens*, *Aeneid* 10.602-4)—a fitting counterpart to Aeneas's first taunt, which threatened that his victim's body would be eaten by fish in a river (*Aeneid* 10.557-60).[40] Camilla's *aristeia* ends with her death, an event through which her essential kinship with the Italian landscape is implied. Specifically, she exhibits qualities of a river:

> simul his dictis linquebat habenas
> **ad terram** non sponte **fluens**. tum frigida toto
> paulatim <u>exsolvit</u> se corpore, <u>lentaque colla</u>
> <u>et captum leto posuit caput</u>, arma relinquens
> vitaque cum gemitu fugit indignata sub umbras.
>
> (Vergil, *Aeneid* 11.827-31)

Just as she said these words, she dropped the reins and **flowed down**, not of her own will, **to the ground**. Then, cold, she gradually <u>loosed</u> herself from her whole body; <u>her neck relaxed and lay down her head, overcome by death</u>; relinquishing her weapons, her life fled, resentful, with a groan to the shades below.

As she flows to the ground, she seems to become part of the natural world. We see a similar sequence of events with another character who represents Italy: Juturna. Although Juturna does not die, she makes her final exit to the underworld by burying herself in the pool named for her (*multa gemens et se fluvio*

---

40. Dyson argues that since there is no river described as being nearby, Vergil means the reader to recall the Homeric parallel (Achilles's threat to Lycaon) and envision a vengeful river (1993, 52).

dea condidit alto, Aeneid 12.886).[41] The way these two Italian characters find a resting place in the landscape via water or the vocabulary of water is similar to the means of Aeneas's apotheosis and thus suggests that, although he is not an Italian, his death signals his acceptance by his new homeland. In particular, the detail of Camilla leaving her body (*exsolvit se corpore*) immediately following the word *fluens* suggests the separation of mortal from immortal in Aeneas at the Numicus.

In addition to their resonances within the *Aeneid*, the lines describing Camilla's death allude to a passage from *Georgics* 3, in which the connection between individual and landscape also is evident. Here an ox, afflicted with the animal plague that dominates the third book of the *Georgics*, finds no solace in the pastoral landscape:

> non umbrae altorum nemorum, non mollia possunt
> prata movere animum, non qui per saxa volutus
> purior electro campum petit amnis; at ima
> solvuntur latera, atque oculos stupor urget inertis
> **ad terramque fluit** devexo pondere cervix.
>
> (Vergil, *Georgics* 3.520-24)

> Neither the shade of tall groves, nor soft meadows were able to move his spirit, nor a stream, more pure than amber, tumbling between rocks, that seeks the field; but his great sides are loosened, and unconsciousness presses his heavy eyes. His neck **flows down to the ground**, its weight brought low.

The plague marks a transition to a harsher and less idyllic time and the death of the ox mirrors the destruction of that way of life. The clearest verbal link between the two passages is the combination of the phrase *ad terram* with a form of the verb *fluere*. The correspondence is strengthened by *exsolvit* and *solvuntur*, as well as the focus on the neck of each victim.[42] Both Camilla and the ox represent an idyllic Italy before the advent of war (or plague) and, as such, they cannot survive the destruction of that landscape. In death, they become part of the natural world physically, transformed metaphorically via water. The sick ox has no interest in his surroundings, including a stream, but as he dies he becomes closer to the land not only through downward motion, but also through the language that describes it (*ad terramque fluit*).

The same thing happens to Camilla (*ad terram non sponte fluens*). The initial tie between this character and river water, however, comes not immediately

---

41. See Dyson 1993, 28, where she also compares *Aeneid* 8.330-32 (the Albula renamed after Tiberinus drowned there). Ovid, too, highlights Juturna's special relationship with the landscape (*Fasti* 2.603).

42. Cf. also the death of Euryalus (*Aeneid* 9.432ff.). His head droops like a poppy in the rain. This image from the natural world is accompanied by specific evocations of water, including *volvitur* (433; see below, ch. 4, for more on this term) and the description of Nisus as similar to a storm (438-43). The language and simile allude to the death of Euphorbus in the *Iliad*. In 16.810ff, Euphorbus kills Patroclus after the two clash like lions fighting over a spring. Euphorbus is then killed by Menelaus in 17.43ff., where Menelaus is compared to a storm.

before her death, but in the description of her childhood. Perhaps the need to direct our gaze so far backward is another reason Vergil recalls the *Georgics* passage at this point: to remind us of an actual river that figures in Camilla's story as well. Indeed, Camilla's father launched her across the river Amasenus tied to a spear (*Aeneid* 11.547-64). This truly proves to be a defining experience for Camilla: not only does it prophesy the advent of war in an idyllic Italy, but the manner of her death echoes the combination of spear and river.

Vergil identifies characters with the landscape via water on another occasion as well. The names of the first two Latin war casualties commemorate the impact of the war on native rivers. The war itself began at a river, where Ascanius shoots Silvia's pet stag (*Aeneid* 7.493-99). Following this incident, Vergil's description of the way news of the war travels uses images of water, as rivers and springs are the entities that hear the Fury's cries with which the woods echo (516-17). Finally, the Trojan forces "stream" from their camp (*effundit*, 522) and the fighting is like an ocean wave (528-30). The names of the first two victims follow immediately:[43]

hic iuvenis primam ante aciem stridente sagitta,
natorum Tyrrhi fuerat qui maximus, Almo
sternitur; haesit enim sub gutture vulnus et udae
vocis iter tenuemque inclusit sanguine vitam.
corpora multa virum circa seniorque Galaesus,
dum paci medium se offert, iustissimus unus
qui fuit Ausoniisque olim ditissimus arvis:
quinque greges illi balantum, quina redibant
armenta, et terram centum vertebat aratris.

(Vergil, *Aeneid* 7.531-39)

At the head of the first battleline, this youth, Almo, who had been the eldest of the sons of Tyrrhus, is laid low by a whistling arrow; for the wound stuck under his throat and it blocked the path of his damp voice and his tender life with blood. Many bodies of men lie around, the old man Galaesus too, while he put himself forth into their midst for peace, Galaesus who was alone the most just man and who once was the richest in Ausonian fields: five flocks of sheep, five herds of cattle returned to him, and he turned the land with a hundred ploughs.

Not only are Almo and Galaesus named for rivers, the language used to describe them exploits this double significance: the phrase *udae vocis* describes Almo breathing his last. Servius explains that his voice is coming through a moist artery,[44] but the detail *udae* could apply to man or river.

The second, Galaesus, is named for the river of Tarentum, near which Vergil locates the Corycian Gardener in *Georgics* 4 and which the Corycian's suc-

---

43. By naming the war's first victims after rivers, Vergil also alludes to the *Iliad*. There Simoesios is one of the first Trojans killed after general fighting breaks out following the duel between Paris and Menelaus (4.473-81).

44. *non enim vox uda est, sed per udam arteriarum labitur viam* (*ad Aeneid* 7.533).

cesses associate with the ideal. The details Vergil provides about Galaesus recall the context in which the name refers to a river. The adjectives *iustissimus* and *ditissimus* recall qualities of the Corycian. Galaesus's agricultural activities are precisely those that the Corycian does not practice, herding and growing large crops (*Georgics* 4.128-29, *Aeneid* 7.538-39), but both men have the same type of success. Galaesus is *ditissimus* (*Aeneid* 7.537) and the Corycian *regum aequabat opes animis* (*Georgics* 4.132). Galaesus is *iustissimus* (*Aeneid* 7.536) and the Corycian's success and contentment recall the happy rustics among whom Justice left her last footprints (*Georgics* 2.467-74).[45] Almo and Galaesus, then, blur the line between characters and landscape. They are, in a sense, rivers that suffer the effects of war in human terms. Camilla, on the other hand, ends her human suffering by taking on the qualities of a river.

Turnus is another Italian character who seems to have a special relationship with the rivers of his native land. One instance in which Turnus's status as a native Italian gives him an advantage over Aeneas prefigures the turning of the tables that will afford Aeneas the same benefit.[46] When Turnus is near defeat at the hands of Aeneas, he leaps into the Tiber:[47]

---

45. Galaesus also evokes the idealized farmer of the *Laudes Italiae* (*Georgics* 2.459-68). The character, in conflating the worlds of the *Eclogues* and *Georgics*, brings to his final Vergilian incarnation a sense that the epic war of the *Aeneid* shatters the worlds and genres of those earlier poems. Other characters, Numanus-Remulus, Camilla, and Faunus, reenact this destruction (Thomas 1992, 69-70).

46. Dyson (1993, 51) sees this passage as an indication that the Italian land still strongly favors Turnus.

47. For the restorative powers of water, cf. the role of Phlegethon in the apotheosis of Hippolytus, as described by Ovid (*Metamorphoses* 15.531-34):

> vidi quoque luce carentia regna
> et lacerum fovi Phlegethontide corpus in unda,
> nec nisi Apollineae valido medicamine prolis
> reddita vita foret

> I also saw the realms lacking in light and I bathed my torn body in Phlegethon's wave,
> nor would life have been returned to me without the sturdy treatment of Apollo's son.

Here, the process has medical connotations because of the association with Aesculepius. The reference to Phlegethon, however, places this example in the context of death, rather than simply of healing. In Propertius, *Elegies* 2.34, Gallus is described in a similar way, although he does not return to life (2.34.91-92):

> et modo formosa quam multa Lycoride Gallus
> mortuus inferna vulnera lavit aqua!

> And now how many wounds from beautiful Lycoris does Gallus, dead, wash in the water of the lower world!

In this passage, the Styx performs the double function of washing as part of funerary ritual and of transporting the deceased to Hades. In Hippolytus's case, the river is not only part of the underworld, but also part of Hippolytus's return to life. Thus, when Turnus leaps into the Tiber, it is a kind of rebirth, and the cleansing he undergoes is more than the literal removal of bloodstains.

tum demum praeceps saltu sese omnibus armis
in fluvium dedit. ille suo cum gurgite flavo
accepit venientem ac mollibus extulit undis
et laetum sociis abluta caede remisit.

(Vergil, *Aeneid* 9.815-18)

Then at last with a leap he gave himself with all his arms to the river. It accepted his coming with its tawny stream and carried him on soft waves and returned him, glad, with the blood washed off, to his companions.

The river washes Turnus's body, although he is not dead. He is, however, at the point of total defeat, which implies imminent death. The Tiber, in saving Turnus, symbolically returns him to life and, by doing so, accomplishes for Turnus a transition from one state of being to another. The idea that Turnus emerges from the river in a changed condition suggests apotheosis. If we foresee Aeneas receiving the same cooperation from an Italian river, we conclude that at that point he, too, will be considered a native.

Given the possibility that rivers may reject foreign corpses in their streams, however, Aeneas is not assured of the reception at the Numicus that Ovid envisions for him. Jupiter's decree that Aeneas will become Indiges (*Aeneid* 12.795) explicitly points to apotheosis as the outcome, but the poem repeatedly makes clear that he is not there yet. Vergil's attention to the poetic tradition in which rivers can respond to death by either mirroring funerary rites or denying burial not only emphasizes the foreign status of the Trojans upon their arrival in Italy, but also shapes our perception of Aeneas's death. Indeed, hints such as these are the only way Vergil has to convey this event that occurs outside the frame of the poem. Indeed, it is significant that Vergil restricts himself to hints. The end of the *Aeneid* leaves us with a sense of loss and only upon further reflection do we see Aeneas's integration not only into the society of the Latins but also, at his death, into the society of the gods and into the landscape itself, via the Numicus river.

Water, specifically river water, has an essential part in ritual observances. Although the rituals in which it appears apply to several distinct aspects of life, they have in common the idea of transition from one state of being to another. Water provides a physical manifestation of metaphysical transformations. Indeed, this notion can apply to the role water plays in ethnographical theories. In ethnography, as in ritual, water can provide an outward manifestation of cultural distinctions that are difficult to visualize.

Chapter Three

Ethnography

In addition to placing themselves in the context of the universe and the gods, the Greeks and Romans understand themselves in the cultural framework of human society. Here too, rivers play a crucial role in defining identity. It has been noted in chapter 1 that various waters were believed to have particular physical properties that could effect changes upon those who came in contact with those waters. All rivers, it seems, have unique properties, although they are often less dramatic. Ethnographers adduce connections between the character of a landscape and the qualities of the people who inhabit it.[1] In ethnographical writings, the characteristics of a local river often show particular similarities to the constitution of those to whom it supplies water.

The principle that people and rivers of the same region have similar characteristics goes back to the Hippocratic *Airs, Waters, Places*. As the work's title suggests, the character of a region's water is one of three major factors that determine the nature of the inhabitants. The author asserts that the water in every place is unique:

> δεῖ δὲ καὶ τῶν ὑδάτων ἐνθυμεῖσθαι τὰς δυνάμιας· ὥσπερ γὰρ ἐν τῷ στόματι
> διαφέρουσι καὶ ἐν τῷ σταθμῷ, οὕτω καὶ ἡ δύναμις διαφέρει πολὺ ἑκάστου.
> (Hippocrates, *Airs, Waters, Places* 1)

> It also is necessary to consider the powers of waters; for just as they differ in taste and in weight, so also the power of each differs much.

The nature of the water contributes not only to the character of a place, but also to the health of those who live there (*Airs, Waters, Places* 7). The author describes various types of water in order from worst to best. The characteristics present in the water tend to be those associated with the people as well. For instance, those who live near marshy, stagnant waters that are hot and thick (θερμὰ καὶ παχέα, *Airs, Waters, Places* 7) in summer and cold and turbid in winter tend to have, among other things, hot, dry digestive organs (ξηροτάτας τε καὶ θερμοτάτας, *Airs, Waters, Places* 7). This descriptive approach uses the

---

1. See Thomas 1982.

principle of like to like to suggest that people and water are suited to one another. At the same time, the author offers a framework within which to view the variety that exists in the world.

In addition to describing the qualities of various waters and peoples, the author treats water as an allopathic remedy. Waters of one type can be used therapeutically to treat maladies associated with other types of water:

> ὅστις δὲ νούσου εἵνεκα βούλεται τὸ ἐπιτηδειότατον πίνειν, ὧδε ἂν ποιέων μάλιστα τυγχάνοι τῆς ὑγιείης· ὁκόσων μὲν αἱ κοιλίαι σκληραὶ εἰσι καὶ συγκαίειν ἀγαθαί, τούτοισι μὲν τὰ γλυκύτατα συμφέρει καὶ κουφότατα καὶ λαμπρότατα· ὁκόσων κὲ μαλθακαὶ αἱ νηδύες καὶ ὑγραί εἰσι καὶ φλεγματ-ώδεες, τούτοισι δὲ τὰ σκληρότατα καὶ ἀτεραμνότατα καὶ τὰ ὑφαλυκά· οὕτω γὰρ ἂν ξηραίνοιντο μάλιστα.
>
> (Hippocrates *Airs, Waters, Places* 7)

One who because of disease wants to drink the most suitable water, doing thus would gain health the most; those whose intestines are hard and have a tendency to become hot, for these men the sweetest and lightest and most sparkling waters are beneficial; those whose stomachs are soft and moist and phlegmatic, for these men the hardest and harshest and saltiest are beneficial; for thus they would be dried up the most.

While those in good health can tolerate a range of waters (*Airs, Waters, Places* 7), it is possible for water to cause illness as well as predispose individuals to certain conditions and also to act as a cure. One of the types of water the author names as potentially harmful is water from a great distance:

> λιθιῶσι δὲ μάλιστα ἄνθρωποι καὶ ὑπὸ νεφριτίδων καὶ στραγγουρίης ἁλίσκ-ονται καὶ ἰσχιάδων, καὶ κῆλαι γίνονται, ὅκου ὕδατα πίνουσι παντοδαπ-ώτατα καὶ ἀπὸ ποταμῶν μεγάλων, ἐς οὓς ποταμοὶ ἕτεροι ἐμβάλλουσι, καὶ ἀπὸ λίμνης, ἐς ἥν ῥεύματα πολλὰ καὶ παντοδαπὰ ἀφικνεῦνται, καὶ ὁκόσοι ὕδασιν ἐπακτοῖσι χρέονται διὰ μακροῦ ἀγομένοισι καὶ μὴ ἐκ βραχέος.
>
> (Hippocrates, *Airs, Waters, Places* 9)

With stones most of all people are seized both by kidney disease and by strangury and by sciatica, and ruptures happen, when they drink many different waters and from large rivers, into which other rivers flow, and from a lake into which many and various streams enter, and as many people as use foreign waters brought from a long distance and not from a short distance.

In this passage the risk factors cited all have to do with the origins of one's drinking water. It seems that the consumption of water from a variety of sources represents impurity, which, in turn produces bodily disruptions. It is not just commingled waters, however, that adversely affect health. The same symptoms plague those who use water brought from a distance. The risks associated with consuming water that comes from far away imply a judgment that, in general, local water is compatible with one's physical characteristics and, thus, promotes health.

Herodotus is aware of this principle and even uses it metaphorically. He follows the principles of ethnography found in the Hippocratic *Airs, Waters, Places* when commenting on the relationship between water and health. In describing the rivers of the Scythians, he includes details of water quality:

ἐκ ταύτης ὧν ἀνατέλλων ὁ ῞Υπανις ποταμὸς ῥέει ἐπὶ μὲν πέντε ἡμερέων πλόον βραχὺς καὶ γλυκύς ἔτι ἀπὸ δὲ τούτου πρὸς θαλάσσης τεσσέρων ἡμερέων πλόον πικρὸς αἰνῶς.
. . .
(σχ. ὁ Βορυσθένης) πίνεσθαί τε ἡδιστός ἐστι, ῥέει τε καθαρὸς παρὰ θολεροῖσι, σπόρος τε παρ ᾽ αὐτὸν ἄριστος γίνεται, ποίη τε, τῇ οὐ σπείρεται ἡ χώρη, βαθυτάτη.

(Herodotus, *History* 4.52, 53)

Issuing forth from this lake, the Hypanis River flows for five days' sail shallow and sweet, but from there to the sea for four days' sail it is terribly brackish.
. . .
(The Dneiper) is sweetest to drink, and it flows clear alongside muddy ones, and the sowing of crops is best beside it, and there is very deep grass, where the land is not sown.

The general qualities of water that Herodotus considers healthful, as well as the specific term γλυκύς, correspond to the Hippocratic author's opinion. In addition to mentioning the characteristics of water compatible with health, implying the Hippocratic like to like principle, Herodotus extends the relationship to non-physical aspects of a culture. He introduces his ethnography of Egypt in the following way:

Αἰγύπτιοι ἅμα τῷ οὐρανῷ τῷ κατὰ σφέας ἐόντι ἑτεροίῳ καὶ τῷ ποταμῷ φύσιν ἀλλοίην παρεχομένῳ ἢ οἱ ἄλλοι ποταμοί, τὰ πολλὰ πάντα ἔμπαλιν τοῖσι ἄλλοισι ἀνθρώποισι ἐστήσαντο ἤθεά τε καὶ νόμους.

(Herodotus, *History* 2.35)

The Egyptians, just as the climate belonging to them is different and their river displays a nature different from other rivers, for the most part they have established customs and laws contrary to other peoples.[2]

In this case, there is no physical reason why the people resemble their river. The unique nature of the Nile, however, provides a useful metaphor for Herodotus's conception of the Egyptians: that their customs invert those of the Greeks.

The identification of rivers with peoples can even extend to river gods. Pausanias and Pliny mention that statues of the Nile were done in black stone. Indeed, Pausanias asserts that this generally was the case:

---

2. See also Herodotus 2.19.

ποιεῖται δὲ πλὴν τοῦ Αἰγυπτίου Νείλου ποταμοῖς τοῖς ἄλλοις λίθου λευκοῦ
τὰ ἀγάλματα· τῷ Νείλῳ δέ, ἅτε διὰ τῆς Αἰθιόπων κατιόντι ἐς θάλασσαν, μέ-
λανος λίθου τὰ ἀγάλματα ἐργάζεσθαι νομίζουσιν.

(Pausanias, *Guide to Greece* 8.24.12)

Statues of rivers other than the Egyptian Nile are made from white stone; but
statues of the Nile, since it flows down to the sea through Ethiopia, are traditionally made from black stone.

While there exist some statues of the Nile in dark marble, there are also representations in white stone.[3] Pliny describes one such statue of the Nile in dark
stone:[4]

invenit eadem Aegyptus in Aethiopia quem vocant basaniten, ferrei coloris
atque duritiae, unde et nomen ei dedit. numquam hic maior repertus est quam in
templo Pacis ab imperatore Vespasiano Augusto dicatus argumento Nili,
sedecim liberis circa ludentibus, per quos totidem cubita summi incrementi
augentis se amnis eius intelleguntur.

(Pliny, *Natural History* 36.11.58)

Also in Ethiopia, the Egyptians discovered what they call "basanites," the color
and hardness of iron, from which it was named. Never was a larger one found
than the one representing the Nile dedicated by the emperor Vespasian in the
temple of Peace, with sixteen children playing around it, through whom the
number of cubits of the highest desirable level of the flood are known.

These statements speak to a desire to assimilate river gods to the people they
represent. The impulse is similar to Herodotus's metaphor of unique river for
unique people. Indeed, representations of barbarians might make use of color to
signify difference. Schneider collects a number of statues in which skin color is
represented by a different color marble than that which is used to sculpt clothing. Statues of barbarians, however, also include examples in which the whole
statue is carved from marble of a single color and details such as dress, hairstyle,
and facial features indicate the subject's status as a foreigner.[5] In these cases, as
with statues of river gods, the color of the stone may, but does not necessarily
have to approximate skin color.

Poets, too, in associating themselves or their characters with locations appropriate to their natures, often choose rivers as a focal point in the landscape.[6]
Victims of love tend to be associated with rivers at the edges of civilization.
Vergil envisions Gallus wandering by the Permessus (*Eclogues* 6.64). He connects Orpheus with both the Strymon and the Tanais (*Georgics* 4.508, 518). The
former, associated with Amazons, alludes to Orpheus's death at the hands of

---

3. Roman statues of river gods in dark marble are collected by Gregarek (1999, 176-77, nos.
A32-A38).
4. See Ostrowski 1991, 12.
5. Schneider 1986, 188-95.
6. See below, ch. 4, for more on rivers as metaphors for poetic composition.

violent women, while the latter emphasizes his isolation. In both cases, the isolation of lost love is expressed as physical distance from civilization.[7]

Rivers also may represent more constructive ideas. In the fourth *Georgic*, the Corycian gardener lives by the Galaesus, which Vergil describes as black:

> namque sub Oebaliae memini me turribus arcis,
> qua niger umectat flaventia culta Galaesus,
> Corycium vidisse senem,
>
> (Vergil, *Georgics* 4.125-27)

> For I remember that I saw under the ramparts of the Oebalian citadel, where the black Galaesus waters tawny fields, a Corycian old man . . .

The adjective, *niger*, may, with *flaventia,* be part of a pair of transferred epithets, since *flaventia* tends to apply to rivers and *niger* to fertile soil.[8] In this way, the pair may contribute to an identification of river with land. The detail may also associate the Galaesus with the fertility of the Nile, given the apparent belief that the Nile was represented in black stone. In addition, Herodotus describes the soil that results from Nile floods as black (*History* 2.12). The reference is appropriate, given the unusual productivity that characterizes the Corycian's land. Although there is nothing to make us suspect that the Corycian himself is of Egyptian origin, his skill as a gardener mirrors the fertilizing power of the river, which is described as watering the fields (*umectat*). In addition, the river may claim some responsibility for the fertility of the land. The adjective *flaventia* applies to the land, although it is a more appropriate description for a river. The transfer of this epithet may be quite purposeful, however. The word may serve to emphasize the mechanism through which the fields become fertile: silt, the substance that makes a river *flavus,* is what makes the riverbanks fertile.[9]

As is evident from ethnographic works as well as poetic and artistic conventions, a great deal of similarity appears to exist between people and the rivers of their territory. A river may serve as an emblem of the landscape and, as such, may advertise the identification of people with place. Like other aspects of ethnography, however, the characteristics of a river may serve to distinguish the inhabitants of a region from outsiders.

Of course, practical issues have a place in this discussion as well. Realistically, a foreigner may have more difficulty than a native in crossing a river because natives have the advantage of familiarity with the river. This certainly is

---

7. In Euripides's *Bacchae*, Pentheus suffers a similar isolation and violent death.

8. On *flavus* as applied to rivers, see ch. 6, "Library Catalogues." Twice in the *Georgics*, Vergil describes soil as *niger* (*Georgics* 2.203, 255).

9. The epithet *niger* also may be a reference to Philetas, who described the Burina (a spring in Cos) as black-rocked (μελαμπέτροιο, fr. 24, Powell 1925). The Philetean word, in turn, is a variation on the Homeric river-epithet μελάνυδρος (Thomas 1992, 42). Other interpretations of *niger* include references to the turbidity of the Galaesus or to its depth (OLD s.v. *niger* 4c; Thomas 1992, 42 n. 21). See also Dunbabin (1947, 93) on the difficulty of identifying the Galaesus with a real river, given the qualities Vergil describes.

the case with Hannibal in Livy. When Hannibal's forces meet Scipio's at the Po, Livy details the difficulties the Carthaginians have crossing the river, while Scipio's troops cross easily. While Scipio's crossing of the Po is portrayed unremarkably as merely one of the events leading up to his address to his troops,[10] Hannibal uses the river in his speech as a reason that his army cannot turn back.[11]

Hannibal's point concerning the Alps is clear: his army crossed them once, with difficulty, and now the river has weakened them. His statement implies that an escape over mountains would be even more difficult than their previous crossing. Hannibal's assertion that the Po is more violent than the Rhône (Livy, *Ab Urbe Condita* 21.43.5) serves to make the same point. Earlier, when the Carthaginians crossed the Rhône, Livy emphasized their losses (21.38.3-5). By saying that the Po is even more dangerous than the Rhône, Hannibal implies that this river crossing would be even more devastating than their last.

The same situation occurs at the Ticinus. Scipio's men cross the river on a bridge of boats, but when Hannibal tries to cross, the Romans have detached one end of the bridge and it has drifted downstream (21.47.3). Claiming that Hannibal could not have crossed the Po, Livy asserts that the Carthaginians had to march two days to a point at which they could ford the river (21.47.6). Hannibal's difficulties typify the very real hazards rivers pose to those unfamiliar with their waters.

Literature and art reflect ethnographical theory in their expressions of concerns regarding the suitability of a new environment to its inhabitants. The connections ancient ethnographers make between peoples and their environments influence visual and verbal metaphor.[12] One of the most obvious contexts is the integration of newcomers into a foreign environment. Most often, these concerns are addressed via the assimilation of a new place to a familiar location. The motivation for this association may relate to the idea that colonization actually contributes to nationalism: when one moves to a new place, there is a need to define what constitutes one's culture.[13] The coins of Magna Graecia, which frequently depict river gods, seem to advertise the merits of the new location, a feature common in European literary descriptions of the New World. In these accounts, the New World often takes on the characteristics of the golden age.[14] In the ancient world, the adaptation of the colonists to their new environment is the primary concern. Interestingly, in the colonization of the Americas, it is how well

---

10. *occupavit tamen Scipio Padum traicere, et ad Ticinum amnem motis castris, priusquam educeret in aciem, adhortandorum militum causa talem orationem est exorsus* (Livy, *Ab Urbe Condita* 21.39.4).

11. *dextra laevaque duo maria claudunt nullam ne ad effugium quidem navem habentes; circa Padus amnis—maior Padus ac violentior Rhodano; ab tergo Alpes urgent, vix integris vobis ac vigentibus transitae* (Livy, *Ab Urbe Condita* 21.43.4-5).

12. For examples of Roman iconographical response to conquest, see Nicolet 1991, 34-47.

13. Kupperman 1995, 11.

14. Mackenthun 1997, 36.

the native population assimilates to the newly arrived colonists that receives comment.[15]

Greek colonies in Magna Graecia frequently formulate colonization in terms of rivers, as is particularly evident from their coinage. This observation is not so unusual in itself, as the colonists may have reacted with particular interest to geography when in a new location. The identity of the rivers depicted, however, proves more puzzling. The Achelous, the river of western Greece that in some instances was synonymous with water itself (e.g., Sophocles, *Fragment* 5; Euripides, *Bacchae* 625; Aristophanes, *Frogs* 351), appears on some coins of Magna Graecia, as do representations of local rivers. This practice may be compared with the custom of portraying Greek gods on coins circulated in distant parts of the Greek world. The latter is a means of disseminating and advertising Greek culture. Likewise, advertising a Greek river on colonial coins may provide a metaphorical connection to the old country.

Many coins from Magna Graecia depict river gods as man-headed bulls. This is the standard iconography of the river god Achelous, but some of the coins identify the figures as local river gods.[16] The reasons for the apparent widespread depiction of Achelous on coins are not clear and may be numerous. Jenkins has noted that depictions of man-headed bulls are plentiful in Etruscan art, although, in this context too, they are derived from Greek art.[17] The cult of Achelous also may contribute to the appearance of this god on coins. It spread from Akarnania to Attica and then beyond Greece to Megara, Mykonos, and Italy.[18] Games in honor of Achelous provide evidence for this spread of cult.[19] Finally we cannot overlook perhaps the simplest explanation: in Greek literature, the name Achelous had become synonymous with water.[20] A water source was essential in choosing a site for a new city, and perhaps it was natural to advertise this important aspect of a location.

---

15. Mackenthun 1997, 146.

16. LIMC s.v. Gelas, Achelous. There are several possible reasons for the man-headed bull as the icon of a river. There seems to have been a longstanding connection between rivers and bulls. In the *Iliad*, the Skamander is said to roar like a bull (21.237). The myth of Herakles includes an account of the shape-shifting Achelous. One form the river god adopts is that of a bull (Sophocles, *Trachiniae* 509-10). In addition to the connection between the force and roaring of a river and the strength and bellowing of a bull, there may be a visual link: the branches of a river may recall the horns of a bull in the same way the moon's crescent or the wings of a battle formation may be referred to as horns (see LSJ s.v. κέρας; OLD s.v. *cornu*). The association of Poseidon, Okeanos, rivers, and bulls is very old (Nagy 1990, 236ff.).

17. Jenkins 1970, 167. See also Mussini 2002, 91-119.

18. Farnell 1909, 5:421.

19. It seems, however, that the evidence is limited to coins and Philostratus's *Heroikos* (Olearius p. 678, l. 21; p. 746, l. 5).

20. *Licet abunde ista sufficient ad probationem moris antiqui, quo ita loquendi usus fuit ut Achelous commune omnis aquae nomen haberetur, tamen his quoque etiam Euripidis nobilissimi tragoediarum scriptoris addetur auctoritas* ... (Macrobius, *Saturnalia* 5.18.11). Additional evidence comes from the works of Euripides and Aristophanes, in which Achelous stands metonymically for water on a number of occasions (Euripides, *Andromache* 167, *Hypsipyle* fragment 753, *Bacchae* 519 and 625; Aristophanes, *Lysistrata* 381, fragment 351).

Aside from these practical reasons for depicting a distant, or at least generic, river on coins, the man-headed bull may serve an allusive function. As a kind of visual "cf.", the Achelous bull may relate rivers of Magna Graecia to those of Greece. This kind of reference may fulfill the same function as naming cities or rivers after those in the place from which the colony set out.[21]

Coins of Magna Graecia also frequently depict river nymphs, often those with a link to a story of colonization.[22] Just as the identification of new rivers with the Achelous invites viewers to connect colony with homeland, the myth of Arethusa provides a narrative expression of that link. In the case of Arethusa, the water in the new place is literally the same, transported from its original location. Indeed, it was believed that a river could travel through another body of water without becoming contaminated. The tale, however, is more than a reporting of a natural phenomenon. It is a model for the event of colonization, an analogue in the natural world for a human activity. Pausanias credits the myth as the motive for colonization, reporting that the story was part of the Delphic oracle that prompted the colonization of Syracuse (*Guide to Greece* 5.7.3).[23] Ovid makes a point of Arethusa's status as a foreigner:

> "Huc hospita veni.
> Pisa mihi patria est et ab Elide ducimus ortus,
> Sicaniam peregrina colo, sed gratior omni
> Haec mihi terra solo est: hos nunc Arethusa penates,
> Hanc habeo sedem."
>
> (Ovid, *Metamorphoses* 5.493-97)

"I have come here as a stranger. Pisa is my homeland and I have my origins in Elis, as a foreigner I inhabit Sicily, but this land is more pleasing to me than every place; I, Arethusa, now have these household gods and this dwelling."

By the end of the passage, however, the nymph has become loyal to her new home. Like a colonist, she came as a foreigner, but has made this new place her permanent home.[24] Such terms as *patria* and *peregrina* evoke the legal status one such as Arethusa would have. The term *penates*, however, places her squarely in a Roman context.

In the ancient world, analysis of the myth tended not toward the cultural but toward the scientific. Rivers that could flow through other bodies of water with-

---

21. Chalcidice, Chalcis (Torone) named from Chalcis in Eubeoa; Megara Hyblaea founded from Megara; Locri Epizephyrii founded from Locris. Kraay also mentions a specific connection for one colony: the residents of Metapontum believed they were related to the Aetolians and so established games in honor of the Aetolian river god Achelous and minted coins bearing his image (1976, 179).

22. See Kraay 1976, 3, 209f. Kraay notes several instances in which Arethusa serves as a model for other female figures. For instance, the nymph Kyme on a Cumaean coin resembles Arethusa, as does a goddess depicted on a coin from Tarsus (1976, 178, 281-82).

23. On Arethusa and colonization, see also Dougherty 1993, 68-69, 146.

24. In this role as newcomer turned native, Arethusa appears on Greek coins from Syracuse (see LIMC s.v. Arethusa).

out losing their own identity were accepted as a scientific phenomenon. Pausanias cites several rivers that flow through lakes or other bodies of water unchanged. [25] He does not distinguish based on distance, noncombination of salt and fresh water, or the crossing of national boundaries. The pertinent feature is that certain waters can retain their purity even when apparently combined with other types of water.

In the *Bacchae*, Euripides uses the concept of a river capable of traveling through the sea for the opposite effect. Rather than a Greek river going to a foreign place, the chorus envisions the Nile bringing its fertilizing waters to Cyprus:[26]

ἱκοίμαν ποτὶ Κύπρον,
νᾶσον τᾶς ᾿Αφροδίτας,
ἵν᾿ οἱ θελξίφρονες νέμον-
ται θνατοῖσιν῞Ερωτες,
Πάφον θ᾿ ἃν ἑκατόστομοι
βαρβάρου ποταμοῦ ῥοαὶ
καρπίζουσιν ἄνομβροι.

(Euripides, *Bacchae* 402-8)

Would that I might go to Cyprus, the island of Aphrodite, where the heart-charming Erotes govern mortals, and Paphos, which the seven-mouthed streams of the barbarian river fertilize without rain.

The chorus wishes for escape to distant places and the introduction of the Nile (βαρβάρου ποταμοῦ, 407) to Paphos renders that location all the more exotic. In addition, there is no better way to water the island of Aphrodite than with the most fertile water in the world, renowned for its fertility.[27] From these examples, it seems that a river that travels to a new place can lend something of its character to its new setting. This idea may contribute to explaining the appearance of the Achelous on coins of Magna Graecia.[28]

Aeneid 3 presents a similar situation, in that new surroundings are understood in terms of familiar places. Helenus and his followers attempt without success to recapture their homeland by naming the topographical features in their new locale after those they knew in Troy. Their settlement is a mere shadow of the great city for which it was named. Their failure may be Vergil's comment on the practice: he favors acknowledging the individual character of

---

25. These include the Nile passing through a lake and the river Jordan passing through a lake called Tiberias (Pausanias, *Guide to Greece* 5.7.4).

26. See Dodds 1977, *ad* 402-16 for various explanations of this property. Callimachus notes a similar phenomenon when he envisions a connection between the Nile and the Inopus on Delos (*Hymns* 3.171, 4.208).

27. E.g., Herodotus, *History* 2.12.

28. Also cf. *Eclogues* 10.1ff, where Arethusa's journey through the sea evokes the transfer of pastoral poetry from Arcadia to Sicily, on which see below, ch. 4.

Italy over making it a replica of Troy (or any other place).[29] The language with
which Aeneas describes the topography of Helenus's city reveals the difficulties:

> procedo et parvam Troiam simulataque magnis
> Pergama et arentem Xanthis cognomine rivum
> agnosco, Scaeaeque amplector limina portae;
> nec non et Teucri socia simul urbe fruuntur.
>
> (Vergil, *Aeneid* 3.349-52)

> I go forth and I recognize a small Troy and a Pergamum imitating the great one
> and a dry river named after Xanthus, and I embrace the thresholds of the
> Scaean gates; and the Trojans at the same time enjoy the friendly city.

Despite Trojan pleasure in this faux-familiarity, the phrase, *arentem . . . rivum*
(350), betrays the essential flaw in this practice. Not only is a dry river something of a contradiction, but the comparison of a stream so small it dries up to
the river Homer calls μέγας ποταμὸς βαθυδίνης (*Iliad* 20.73) seems out of pro-
portion.

Livy, too, reveals that he estimates Aeneas's achievement as greater than
that of Antenor, who, like Helenus, founds a new Troy:

> et in quem primum egressi sunt locum Troia vocatur, pagoque inde Troiano
> nomen est: gens universa Veneti appellati. Aenean ab simili clade domo pro-
> fugum, sed ad maiora rerum initia ducentibus fatis, primo in Macedoniam
> venisse, inde in Siciliam quaerentem sedes delatum, ab Sicilia classe ad
> Laurentem agrum tenuisse. Troia et huic loco nomen est.
>
> (Livy, *Ab Urbe Condita* 1.1)

> And the place to which he first went out is called Troy, and from there comes
> the name of the Trojan district: the whole race is called Venetian. Aeneas was
> exiled from home by a similar misfortune, but with the fates leading him to
> greater beginnings of things, first he came to Macedonia, then seeking a home
> he was carried to Sicily, from Sicily the fleet occupied the Laurentian territory.
> Troy also is the name of this place.

Aeneas's destiny (*ad maiora rerum initia*) involves establishing a new people by
overcoming a variety of challenges, while Antenor's peaceful founding of another Troy falls short of this ideal. Indeed, the Troy that Aeneas founds is but
one stage of his journey. It still remains to unite his people with the Latins. He
follows the fates to this final destination after realizing that the intermediate
settlements were not fated for him.

As is evident from the *Aeneid*, colonization can have its pitfalls. Successful
integration into a new homeland is far from assured and, to secure a prosperous

---

29. On renaming, see Buchheit 1963. Callimachus paired the process with city founding, as
evidenced by his "Foundations and renamings of islands and cities," of which only the title remains.
On this work and on Buthrotum as a foundation that does not revive Troy's glory, see Jones 1995
234, 239.

outcome, various conditions must be met. These may be expressed in physical terms: the physical health of individuals as they depend on new resources in their environment indicates the health of the community. Whether the environment itself seems amenable to the new inhabitants also measures the success of the colony.

As we have seen, a shared water source indicates a shared culture. The river from which one drinks is convenient shorthand for the group to which one belongs. The river also shares in the identity of those it nourishes. People and water have essential characteristics in common. The river, however, divides as well as connects. An unfamiliar river may not have properties compatible with those of new inhabitants and yet it may be the path on which those newcomers enter their new environment. In this way, rivers understood in an ethnographical context share in the idea that a river not only establishes a distinction between one group or state of being and another but also provides a means of connection, something that can represent the ties within a group or that can transform colonists from visitors to inhabitants.

The examples presented above demonstrate the main cultural contexts in which rivers occur. They are associated with the origin and formation of the cosmos, with metaphysical transitions, and with ethnographical theories. Human interaction with rivers contributes to defining identity with respect to society, the gods, and the universe/time. All of these ideas are related to the essential function of rivers as connectors but also as boundaries. They may distinguish between two states of being, but they also provide the transition between those states, thus linking them. The remainder of this work will examine the interaction of poetry and art with rivers, specifically rivers that appear in self-referential contexts and elucidate the relationship of artist to art.

Part II

Rivers in a Literary Environment

Chapter Four

The River that Talks:
Rivers and Poetic Speech

Rivers that speak have the potential to be identified with the poet. By gaining a poetic voice, a river can take an active role in a poem's self-referential commentary. The most obvious way in which to achieve this sort of involvement is to use a river god as a narrator. In addition, by placing words in the spatial context of a landscape feature, the author invites comparison of content and form. As we shall see, Vergil employs these devices in the *Eclogues*, *Georgics*, and *Aeneid*, whether to reflect the omniscient status of the poet or to underscore the primacy of poetic ability in a landscape created by the author.

The Rhetoric of Rivers

Writers on rhetoric attribute to their craft a divine or magical element by which properly arranged words elicit emotional responses from an audience or exert their persuasive power on those who hear them.[1] The ordering and presentation of words is the key to transforming language into persuasion.[2] One of the most important characteristics for rhetoric is continuity or flow. To be persuasive, a piece of rhetoric must lead the audience on a predetermined path, much like the course of a river. In addition, the rhetorician must control the way in which the audience encounters the argument: his words must flow past with the correct pacing, much like the current of a river. Rhetoricians frequently use the river as an analogy for their compositions. They recognize that the flow may have different qualities that correspond to different types of watercourses. For Quintilian, a continuous stream is better than a broken one:

---

1. Segal 1962, 121-22.
2. In this respect, rhetorical prose has much in common with poetry, which itself is connected with magic (de Romilly 1975, 8, 11, 16). De Romilly detects what she calls a "liturgical style" in Gorgias's prose (1975, 18).

ceterum quanto vehementior fluminum cursus est prono alveo ac nullas moras
obiciente quam inter obstantia saxa fractis aquis ac reluctantibus, tanto quae
conexa est et totis viribus fluit fragosa atque interrupta melior oratio.

> (Quintilian, *Institutio Oratoria* 9.4.7)[3]

But just as the current of rivers is stronger when the bed slopes and offers no
obstacles than when the waters crash among obstructing rocks and struggle, so
speech that is continuous and flows with every strength is better than that
which is rough and broken off.

The extended river metaphor (*fluminum, alveo, aquis, fluit*) defines good oratorical style as that which flows without interruption or violent changes of pace.
In this assessment, we recognize the defining characteristics of a river: a fluid
substance and motion. For Quintilian, the ideal speech conforms to this definition. Other features a river might possess, such as rocky terrain in its path, are
specifically excluded, leaving an image of motion with underlying continuity.[4]
By removing the hallmarks of a real river (irregular obstructions and changes of
pace), Quintilian abstracts the river just as Heraclitus had in envisioning a watercourse as a model for the cosmos.

The metaphorical river, however, is not a complete abstraction. Both Quintilian and Seneca relate ideal oratory to one type of river in particular. They ad-
vocate endowing the stream of a particular oratorical style with the power of a
mighty river, lest the orator mistake a flowing style for rhetoric that is too gen-
tle:

(sc. eloquentia) feratur ergo non semitis sed campis, non ut ieiuni fontes an-
gustis fistulis colliguntur, sed ut beatissimi amnes totis uallibus fluunt, ac sibi
viam, si quando non acceperit, faciat.

> (Quintilian, *Institutio Oratoria* 5.14.31)[5]

Therefore let eloquence be carried not by paths but by plains, not as poorly fed
springs are gathered in narrow pipes, but as abundant streams flow in entire
valleys; and if ever it does not receive a path, let it make its own.

Here, Quintilian does not contradict what he had said about the necessity of flow
in oratory; rather, he appeals to another aspect of the watercourse, volume, in
order to emphasize force in rhetoric. He does not press the analogy too far: rivers that flow copiously and carve out beds for themselves often are seasonal and

---

3. Cf. Quintilian, *Institutio Oratoria* 12.2.11 for a similar image.

4. Similarly, in *Epistles* 100.1, Seneca praises a consistency of style with a river image. Seneca
recommends speech that flows naturally without apparent artifice. Cicero, too, recognizes flowing
speech as distinct from an interrupted stream of words (*Orator* 53). One cause of a style that does
not flow is an excess of *sententiae* (*Brutus* 325).

5. Cf. Seneca, *Epistles* 115.18.

thus inconstant. Quintilian does not incorporate this consideration into his analogy, but imagines only consistent abundance.[6]

A river that behaves realistically when used in an analogy has a comic effect. Aristophanes implies that a torrent of eloquence, just like a real flood, may dry up:

εἶτα Κρατίνου μεμνημένος, ὃς πολλῷ ῥεύσας ποτ' ἐπαίνῳ
διὰ τῶν ἀφελῶν πεδίων ἔρρει, καὶ τῆς στάσεως παρασύρων
ἐφόρει τὰς δρῦς καὶ τὰς πλατάνους καὶ τοὺς ἐχθροὺς προθελύμνους·
ᾆσαι δ' οὐκ ἦν ἐν συμποσίῳ πλήν· Δωροῖ συκοπέδιλε,
καὶ τέκτονες εὐπαλάμων ὕμνων· οὕτως ἤνθησεν ἐκεῖνος.
νυνὶ δ' ὑμεῖς αὐτὸν ὁρῶντες παραληροῦντ' οὐκ ἐλεεῖτε,

(Aristophanes, *Knights* 526-31)

Then thinking of Cratinus, who, flowing with much praise, coursed across the level plains, and sweeping them from their positions he carries off oaks, planes, and enemies by their roots; at a symposium nothing was sung except "Doro the Fig-Sandaled" and "Contrivers of Inventive Songs"; thus that man flourished. But now, when you see him talking nonsense, you do not pity him,

The description of Cratinus begins with a familiar enough metaphor, πολλῷ ῥεύσας, but continues with a specificity that is at once comical in itself and also suggestive of the outcome. A flood that uproots trees and sweeps people away implies not only a speaking style that is unpleasantly forceful, but one that eventually subsides, as his eloquence falters with age.

River metaphors are not only about style, however. In addition, aspects of oratory such as the structure of argument find expression in terms of rivers:

urgent universa: at singula quaeque dissolueris, iam illa flamma, quae magna congerie convaluerat, diductis quibus alebatur concidet, ut si vel maxima flumina in rivos <diducantur> qualibet transitum praebent.

(Quintilian, *Institutio Oratoria* 5.13.13)

The whole carries great weight: but if you take things individually, they will be like a flame that, having grown strong through its great mass, will collapse when the things that nourished it are removed, just as if even the greatest rivers should be divided into channels, they would offer a crossing at any point.

In this case, a whole argument is like a river that can be divided into channels (or individual points) in order to make crossing (or understanding) easier. The two analogies share the element of human ingenuity. Here, Quintilian stresses the agency of the orator in directing a stream of words, while elsewhere he asserts that everything we say derives (*fluere*) from facts, as if they constitute the source from which a river of words emanates (*Institutio Oratoria* 6.2.13).

---

6. Content, however, must not be lacking. Demosthenes recounts Pytho's failure to persuade despite θρασυνομένῳ καὶ πολλῷ ῥέοντι (*De Corona* 136).

From the general to the specific, types of rivers may represent particular genres or authors as well as aspects of style and structure. In book 10, Quintilian associates several authors with rivers. Whether, like Herodotus, an author simply follows the general guidelines of good rhetoric (*leniter fluunt*, 9.4.18) or, like Lysias, is identified with a particular type of water (*fonti*, 10.1.78), each of these types of writing is in some way similar to flowing water. The analogy of the river for rhetoric extends beyond the classical world: Eduard Norden's own prose reproduces the tendency of ancient literary critics to link authors to watercourses when he describes Isocrates's style as similar to a river. The attributes with which he credits Isocrates (a calm stream flowing over even ground) recall Quintilian's description of good oratory.[7]

Callimachus and the Hesiodic Tradition

Poets, too, see genres and authors as represented by various types of rivers. Not surprisingly, some of the same analogies occur, but as part of a different system of values. Rather than describing a flow of words like a mighty river as ideal, poets like Callimachus associate that sort of writing with epic and they desire for themselves a smaller stream. Apollo himself recommends:

> "Ἀσσυρίου ποταμοῖο μέγας ῥόος, ἀλλὰ τὰ πολλά
> λύματα γῆς καὶ πολλὸν ἐφ' ὕδατι συρφετὸν ἕλκει.
> Δηοῖ δ' οὐκ ἀπὸ παντὸς ὕδωρ φορέουσι μέλισσαι,
> ἀλλ' ἥτις καθαρή τε καὶ ἀχράαντος ἀνέρπει
> πίδακος ἐξ ἱερῆς ὀλίγη λιβὰς ἄκρον ἄωτον."
>
> (Callimachus, *Hymn* 2.107-12)

"The Assyrian river's stream is great, but it carries in its water much silt and rubbish. The Melissae bring water to Deo not from every spring, but from the one that trickles pure and undefiled, a minute stream from a sacred fountain, the absolute finest."[8]

Callimachus focuses on another characteristic of large rivers that Quintilian overlooks: the tendency for the water to become muddied. The equation of a mighty river with prolific verbal production is understood, but, for Callimachus, volume comes with a price: quality. Because he sees small-scale poetry as superior in quality to epic, he depicts large rivers as muddy, carrying excess material in their flow. Purity is the hallmark of the small spring or rivulet, which here receives the additional compliment of religious importance and, thus, divine favor.

---

7. "Wie ein ruhiger Fluß gleitet er auf ebenem Terrain breit dahin: es gibt keine Berge zu durchbrechen, sondern sanfte Hügelketten begleiten ihn während der ganzen Dauer seines Laufes auf beiden Seiten" (Norden 1923, 114. See also Quintilian, *Institutio Oratoria* 10.1.61 and 10.1.94 on Horace.

8. Cf. Horace, *Satires* 1.4.9-13, referring to the writings of earlier satirists such as Lucilius.

The association of epic with a large yet muddy river and Callimachean poetry with a pure spring became a *topos*. Ovid demonstrates his knowledge of the convention and produces his own variation. Pressing the idea that smaller is better to its logical conclusion, Ovid describes his own poetic flow becoming problematically narrow. The flow may become too small, however, as Ovid finds. He likens the difficulty of writing poetry while in exile to a spring obstructed by silt (*Epistles from Pontus* 4.2.15-20). Rather than introducing impurities, Ovid's silt diminishes his poetry, rendering it not λεπτός but *pauper*. The topographical metaphor, although it recalls the Callimachean topos, may also indicate the unsuitability of Ovid's new environment in Tomis for poetic endeavor. At the same time, there is an implied connection between the quality of Ovid's poetry/spring and the poet's health. *Venas* in line 17 clearly refers to water channels, but *vena* in line 20 blurs the line between poet and spring: there the term references the "channels" of the poet's *pectora* that have been silted by his misfortunes.

River analogies, whether in prose or poetry, have a consistent relationship to genre, despite the differing value judgments present in those forms. Large rivers correspond to prolific or forceful writing and small ones to works on a smaller scale. Poets, however, envision another, more direct interaction with water: it can serve as a means of inspiration. The poet attains this inspiration by approaching a particular spring or by drinking its water.

Just as a spring is the source of a river, the water of poetically significant springs may be seen as the source of a poet's creative flow. Hesiod speaks of the springs on Mount Helicon as involved in his inspiration. Subsequent poets, such as Callimachus, wishing to write in the same vein, recall that scene (*Aetia,* fragments 2, 112). Roman poets frequently describe the process of inspiration as one of drinking from the appropriate spring. Just as physical effects result from the consumption of various waters, inspiration or artistic influence may result from association with a famous spring. Through this belief, certain springs acquire a poetic genealogy. As a result, they come to be used as a kind of shorthand in which the name of a spring refers readers to a genre or to the works of a particular poet.

The springs of Mount Helicon come to represent Hesiod. While Hesiod does not mention drinking from particular springs as a source of poetic inspiration, he does connect his poetry indirectly with his local water. Since he reports that his home is Ascra on the slopes of Mount Helicon (*Works and Days* 640), presumably the springs on the mountain were the source of his drinking water. It is left to later poets, however, to make that connection. Hesiod begins his *Theogony* with the Muses, his inspiration. Before they can begin their song, however, they dance and then bathe in the springs of Helicon, Permessus, Hippocrene, and Olmeus (*Theogony* 1-11). Once they reach the summit of the mountain, they begin their song with Zeus. The presence of the Muses on Mount Helicon confirms that place and poet meet their standard.

The image of Hesiod imbibing inspirational waters, however, has its origin in the Alexandrian imagination. The rise of ethnography as a discipline in the years between Hesiod and the Hellenistic poets may have something to do with this development.[9] As we have seen, the Hippocratic *Airs, Waters, Places* links characteristics of peoples to the waters of their native lands. Asclepiades envisions the Muses serving water to Hesiod from Helicon's springs (*Palatine Anthology* 9.64.5-8). As in Hesiod, the Muses still play a role, but Antipater of Sidon presents the transfer of inspiration from Muses to poet in physical terms: the poet must ingest something. The nature of the water, too, is important. In addition to the location of the spring, the water may have qualities that suggest it as a catalyst to poetic endeavor. Antipater of Sidon characterizes the water of Helicon that Hesiod drank as ὕδωρ / εὐεπὲς (*Palatine Anthology* 11.24.1-2). This water that is good for words recalls the Hippocratic recommendations of types of water to influence health (*Airs, Waters, Places* 7).

Poets also may absorb genre via water. By claiming to drink from another poet's spring, a writer may share in that poet's sensibilities and talents. Moschus presents Bion as preferring to drink from Arethusa (*Epithphios Bionis* 71-84). Since Bion favors the pastoral genre, he must go far afield, despite living in Smyrna near the river Meles, which Moschus implies was Homer's local water source. Arethusa, on the other hand, is in Sicily, home of the pastoral hero Daphnis. In ethnographical literature, the river from which one draws water is one way of identifying an individual (see above, chapter 3). Poets use this relationship to associate themselves with not only influential authors but also genres, which often have a geographical affiliation.

The Poet's Draught: Water and Inspiration in Rome

Vergil's *Eclogues* and to some extent his *Georgics* engage Hellenistic notions of water and poetic inspiration as well as the analogy between flowing water and continuous words.

In Roman literature, the springs of Helicon signal not only Hesiod but also his Hellenistic followers. In *Eclogue* 6, Silenus describes Gallus wandering beside the Permessus before ascending to the top of Helicon. Clausen reads this passage as a reference by Vergil to the topography of Mount Helicon, where the Permessus is in the valley, while the other springs are closer to the summit.[10] When Gallus abandons the Permessus, he leaves behind love elegy for a higher genre, aetiological poetry, meaning his poem on the Grynean Grove.[11] Propertius had linked the Permessus with elegy and Helicon with Hesiodic epic (*Elegies* 2.10.25-26). In addition, the upward progress follows Hesiod's Muses, who proceed from bathing in the springs to dance on Helicon's highest slopes. When

---

9. Pindar is the first to associate inspiration and drinking from a fountain (*Olympian* 6.84-88). For Pindar, Thebe, a local spring, provides the poet's drinking water. Although Pindar does not identify the water as the direct cause of his poetic inspiration, temporal coincidence implies a causal relationship.

10. Indeed, topographically this is the case. For a thorough examination of the locations of the springs and rivers on Mount Helicon, see Wallace 1974, 5-24.

11. Clausen 1995, *ad Eclogue* 6.64.

Gallus achieves this elevation, the Muses give him Hesiod's reed pipe (*Eclogue* 6.69-70).[12] Ross, however, does not see a distinction between the Permessus and Helicon, both of which, for Hesiod, are part of the same landscape. Thus, when Vergil invokes these places, he recognizes Gallus as a poetic descendant of both Hesiod and Callimachus.[13] Ross's argument, that for Vergil genealogy trumps genre when evaluating a poet's work, greatly illuminates *Eclogue* 6, but the geographical distinction between the Permessus and Helicon's loftier springs need not be discounted. By ascending Helicon, Gallus may seem to bring his poetic inheritance back to its source, perhaps by rediscovering the tradition's unifying aspect, with which Ross credits him.[14]

It is also in Roman poetry that the idea of inspiration through drinking water from poetically significant springs gains its greatest prominence.[15] For Propertius, water is crucial in his attempt to capture a poetic genre or style. In 3.1, Propertius inquires of Callimachus and Philitas what water they drank, presumably so that he can drink it as well (1-6). Conversely, the poet must avoid some water. In 3.3, Propertius dreams that he has the opportunity to drink from Hippocrene and thus to write epic, but Apollo advises him to seek another water source. Even before the god's intervention, however, Propertius seems ill-suited to the waters of Hippocrene. The spring is described as great (*magnis . . . fontibus*) while the poet's mouth is small (*parva . . . ora*). The solution involves a suitable spring to which Calliope directs the poet.[16] Rather than the name of a spring, we learn only the name of another poet to imbibe the water that now nourishes Propertius's creativity: Philitas, whom Propertius expressed a desire to emulate in 3.1. Thus, 3.3 provides an answer to the question posed in 3.1.6 and an end to the poet's search for inspirational water, a conclusion we may view as a renewed commitment to the poetic values advertised in the book's first poem.

Knowing the identity of inspirational water is not all that matters, however. In Roman poetry, at least, the act of drinking also plays an important role. Cameron privileges the water itself over the act of drinking in descriptions of poets inspired by springs.[17] Lucilius and Lucretius, however, present the act of drinking as an analogy for the reception of poetic ability or even for specific subject matter:

> quod si pigaris paulumve recesseris ab re,
> hoc tibi de plano possum promittere, Memmi:
> usque adeo largos haustus e fontibus magnis
> lingua meo suavis diti de pectore fundet,

---

12. Propertius agrees with Vergil that the Permessus is a source of modest inspiration (*Elegies* 2.10.25-26).

13. Ross 1975, 33-34.

14. Ross 1975, 38.

15. See Wimmel 1960, 222-37.

16. Ovid similarly considers Castalia an appropriate spring to inspire his poetry (*Amores* 1.15.35-38). The waters of Pieria, however, are associated with epic (*Amores* 3.9.25-26; Lucretius, *De Rerum Natura* 927).

17. Cameron 1995, 364-65.

ut verear ne tarda prius per membra senectus
serpat et in nobis vitai claustra resolvat,
quam tibi de quavis una re versibus omnis
argumentorum sit copia missa per auris.

(Lucretius, *De Rerum Natura* 1.410-17)[18]

But if you grow tired or retreat a little from the matter, I can surely promise you
this, Memmius: my pleasing tongue will pour from my rich breast such vast
draughts from great fountains, that I fear slow old age may creep through my
limbs and loosen the bonds of my life sooner than my wealth of versified ar-
guments on some individual point has entered your ears.

Here, Lucretius makes drinking a model for the way he uses his sources. As he
experiences other compositions, they influence his own writing. Thus, it is clear
that not only is the specific spring with which a poet is associated important, but
also the act of drinking. This principle, that water can produce effects in the
drinker, recalls the principle that certain waters, when consumed, produce various physical effects. Theories of water that has the ability to transform those
who drink it existed in both Greece and Rome, but for the Romans there was an
added link to poetry: the Camenae.

For Roman writers, inspirational springs and Muses merge. *Camenae*, the
earliest translation of Μοῦσαι into Latin, signifies a group of water nymphs
associated with a grove and spring outside the Porta Capena (Plutarch, *Life of
Numa* 13).[19] While the Camenae often simply stand in for the Greek Muses,[20] the
title may retain some association with water. Frontinus, in fact, mentions the
Camenae solely as water divinities:[21]

fontium memoria cum sanctitate adhuc exstat et colitur; salubritatem aegris
corporibus afferre creduntur, sicut Camenarum et Apollinis et Iuturnae. nunc
autem in urbem influunt aqua Appia, Anio Vetus, Marcia, Tepula, Iulia, Virgo,
Alsietina quae eadem vocatur Augusta, Claudia, Anio Novus.

(Frontinus, *On Aqueducts* 4)

Regard for springs still continues and is observed with veneration. They are
believed to bring healing to the sick, as, for example, the springs of the Camenae, of Apollo, and of Juturna. But now the following run into the city: the
Appian aqueduct, the Old Anio, Marcia, Tepula, Julia, Virgo, Alsietina, which
also is called Augusta, Claudia, and New Anio.

---

18. See also Lucilius, *Fragments* 1008 M, 1061 W and Lucretius, *De Rerum Natura* 1.927-28,
4.2-3.

19. Livius Andronicus uses the term in his translation of Homer's *Odyssey* (*Virum mihi, Ca-
mena, insece versutum, Odyssia* 1.1).

20. E.g. Horace, *Odes* 1.12.42, 3.4.21, 3.4.36, 4.9.8; *Carmen Saeculare* 62; *Epistles* 1.1.1,
1.18.47, 1.19.5; *Ars Poetica* 275; Propertius, *Elegies* 3.10.1; Ovid, *Fasti* 3.275, 4.245, *Metamorphoses* 14.434, 15.482, *Epistles from Pontus* 4.13.33.

21. See below for possibly pointed references by Vergil and Horace.

Here, Frontinus juxtaposes natural springs with man-made aqueducts, thus implying that these new waters add to the benefits enjoyed by the city that is fortunate enough to have several healthful springs. Frontinus contends that awareness of Rome's springs persists (*memoria . . . exstat*). He implies that his own work may achieve a similar status for aqueducts. In this way, watercourses, whether natural or artificial, may inspire writers, whether as Muses or as subjects for literary endeavors.

The mythology of the Camenae also suggests their involvement with poetic endeavors. Plutarch implies that they are involved in prophecy. When Rome is suffering from a plague, Numa learns from Egeria and the Camenae that a bronze shield that fell from the sky will insure the salvation of the city (*Life of Numa* 13). Although Plutarch refers to the goddesses as Muses, it is clear from the consecration of their spring for the use of the Vestals that these divinities are the Camenae.

The ability of water gods to be both element and anthropomorphic divinity is also at work in the case of the Camenae. Although they are goddesses and Muses, the Camenae also function as spring water. Drinking, then, is the best way for a poet to receive their inspiration.[22] This means of transferring poetic inspiration was not the invention of those who invoked the Camenae, but through their writings it gained its greatest currency.

Rivers and Authorial Mediation in the *Eclogues* and *Georgics*

For Vergil, water represents not only a starting point for inspiration, but also closure. Whereas poetic inspiration often is envisioned as a stream that affects the poet, subsequent aspects of the poetry, such as genre and closure, are represented as a watercourse governed by the poet. This mediation of poetry by the poet suggests a vision of poetic composition that places the poet between inspiration and audience. The issue of closure, of reining in the flow of a narrative, captures the attention of poet and reader in *Eclogue* 3. Perhaps self-conscious that this has been the longest of the *Eclogues*, Vergil closes the poem with a reference to satiety:

> non nostrum inter vos tantas componere lites:
> et vitula tu dignus et hic, et quisquis amores
> aut metuet dulcis aut experietur amaros.
> claudite iam rivos, pueri; sat prata biberunt.
>
> (Vergil, *Eclogue* 3.108-11)

It is not mine to decide such contests: both you and he deserve the calf, as does whoever fears sweet loves or tastes bitter ones. Now close the irrigation ditches, boys; the fields have drunk enough.

---

22. Drinking water for inspiration may be contrasted with drinking wine. The contrast often runs along generic lines. See Knox 1985, 107-19.

These lines, spoken by Palaemon, mediator of the singing contest that occupies most of this poem, merge poet and speaker through their common role as arbiters of words. The lines also relate poetry to farming. Like the farmer who dictates the opening and closing of irrigation channels, the poet is responsible for beginning and ending his poem, a task he may accomplish through the characters who speak the lines, figures analogous to the *pueri* commanded to close the channels in line 111. In both poetry and farming, moderation is essential: doing too much or too little causes poems and crops to fail. The coincidence of the conclusion of the poem with the end of the singing contest calls attention to the artful way in which the irrigation metaphor signals the end in both inner and outer frames.[23]

Indeed, references to water and art unite the inner and outer frames of the poem in other places as well, making the final equation of stream and narrative a fitting coda. In addition to concluding both poem and shepherds' songs, Palaemon introduces the contest, providing a transition from Menalcas's and Damoetas's conversation to their songs and from outer to inner frame. In this introduction, Palaemon's reference to the Camenae prefigures the connections between water and poetry that will surface in the shepherds' songs and in Palaemon's final line.[24]

Connections between poetry and water seem to continue in the shepherds' songs themselves. Menalcas and Damoetas interrupt their discussion of good and bad poets to warn their flocks away from a swift-flowing stream and advise Tityrus that springs are safer for flocks than rivers (*Eclogue* 3.94-97). Following a comparison of poets with a contrast between river water and spring water suggests the Callimachean comparison of epic to a large river and of refined poems to a pure spring.[25] The contrast between Damoetas and Tityrus as goatherds parallels that between Pollio on the one hand and Bavius and Maevius on the other as good and bad poets.

These comparisons between poetry and farming are part of a tendency in *Eclogue* 3 toward spatial representations of poetry or language that serve to connect inner and outer frames. This tendency is evident in the riddles posed by Menalcas and Damoetas (104-7). Damoetas asks where the expanse of the sky occupies only five feet. Menalcas replies with an equally cryptic riddle, asking where flowers grow inscribed with the names of kings. Hofmann proposes that the answers to both riddles may be literary locations (papyrus rolls containing the poetry of Aratus and Euphorion) and that these allusions connect with the literary associations of the cups described in lines 35-47.[26] In addition, the first

---

23. Other *Eclogues* also note their own conclusions: 2, 6, and 10 conclude with the end of the day (Clausen 1995, *ad Eclogue* 3.111). *Eclogue* 3, however, is the only one to imply human mediation as the deciding factor.

24. As we have seen, *Camenae* often implies no more than *Musae*, but Vergil uses the term only here. Nevertheless, Horace makes the Camenae an emblem of Vergil's rustic poetry (*Satires* 1.10.4-5).

25. Callimachus, *Hymn* 2.108-12.

26. Hofmann 1985, 468-80.

riddle expresses a relationship between nature and the written word and the second riddle inverts that relationship: Aratus's *Phaenomena* puts nature into writing while the hyacinth flower is an example of written letters occuring in nature.[27] Palaemon then caps this image with his final lines, representing the singing contest and the entire poem as flowing water and thus putting poetry into a spatial context.

While the irrigation ditches at the end of the third *Eclogue* emphasize closure, flowing water can also make for an equivocal conclusion. Such an ending characterizes the death of Orpheus in *Georgics* 4. There, while the singer dies, both song and river go on:

> tum quoque marmorea caput a cervice revulsum
> gurgite cum medio portans Oeagrius Hebrus
> volveret, Eurydicen vox ipsa et frigida lingua,
> a miseram Eurydicen! anima fugiente vocabat:
> Eurydicen toto referebant flumine ripae.
>
> (Vergil, *Georgics* 4.523-27)

> Even then, when Oeagrian Hebrus rolled the head, plucked from its marble-white neck and carried it in the middle of the stream, the voice itself and the cold tongue cried, "Eurydice, ah, miserable Eurydice!" as life fled: the banks of the entire river echoed "Eurydice."

The Hebrus carries Orpheus's head as it speaks and joins in his lament by echoing his words with its banks, its flow mirroring Orpheus's continued words. The verb that expresses the river carrying Orpheus's head, *volveret* (525), recalls *evolvisse* (507), the word used to describe Orpheus's lament in the underworld. Indeed, *volvo* and *evolvo* can refer to the act of telling a story or reading a papyrus scroll.[28] By selecting this term to describe the river carrying Orpheus's head, Vergil underlines the parallelism between Orpheus's song and the river's flow: both are continuous and independent of human life. Unlike the poetry in *Eclogue* 3, Orpheus's song is not mediated, but has its own existence in the same way that a river differs from an irrigation channel.

In *Eclogue* 3 and *Georgics* 4, the end of a poem or the death of a character affords the poet an opportunity to comment, through reference to moving water, on the dynamic quality of words. Likewise, a beginning can offer such an opportunity. In *Georgics* 3.1-48, the proem to the second half of the work, Vergil makes pointed reference to flowing water. The poet envisions a future literary

---

27. This is analogous to the situation in the ecphrases. In *Eclogue* 3, the ecphrases describe works of art that, in turn, describe poetry (if indeed we are to see Aratus through mention of the *arator* [43] and Euphorion through reference to Orpheus [46] as Hofmann [1985, 475-76] suggests). These poetic figures are the centerpieces of the cups on which they appear and they dominate the composition (Thomas 1983a, 178).

28. *Evolvo* also describes the deeds of Turnus, envisioned in written form (*Aeneid* 9.525-28). Cicero uses *evolutio* to denote the act of reading (*De Finibus* 1.25). *Volvo* also applies to papyrus rolls in Vergil (*Aeneid* 1.262). *Evolvo* and *volvo* also apply to rivers in Vergil: *evolvo* to the Xanthus in *Aeneid* 5.807-8 and *volvo* to the Eridanus in *Aeneid* 6.659 and the Tiber in *Aeneid* 8.539.

work as a temple to Octavian, again lending words spatial reality (12-18).[29] The location of the temple, however, is as significant as its presence or role in celebrating Octavian. By positioning the structure of his poetry beside the Mincius River, Vergil includes the dynamic as well as the monumental in his description. The description of the river exhibits topographical accuracy,[30] but the vocabulary Vergil uses to evoke the broad, reed-lined river suggests a symbolic value as well. Wimmel has noted the similarity between two aspects of Vergil's Mincius and the two genres Callimachus compares in *Hymn* 2.[31] His case centers on the adjectives *ingens* (14) and *tenera* (15), which imply that Vergil's anticipated poem will be an epic (as represented by the large river) but with a Callimachean sensibility (indicated by the delicate reeds along the banks).

On two other occasions, Vergil describes the Mincius in the context of poetry. In *Eclogue* 7.12, he describes bees living near the Mincius and, in *Georgics* 2.199, swans.[32] The wording of *Georgics* 3.15 recalls these prior passages, suggesting that poetic associations are appropriate here as well:

> tardis ingens ubi flexibus errat
> Mincius et tenera praetexit harundine ripas.

> (Vergil, *Georgics* 3.14-15)

. . . where the great Mincius wanders with its leisurely bends and clothes his banks with the delicate reed.

> et qualem infelix amisit Mantua campum
> pascentem niveos herboso flumine cycnos:

> (Vergil, *Georgics* 2.198-99)

. . . and such a plain as unfortunate Mantua lost, as it fed snow-white swans with its grassy stream . . .

> hic viridis tenera praetexit harundine ripas
> Mincius, eque sacra resonant examina quercu.

> (Vergil, *Eclogue* 7.12-13)

Here Mincius clothes his banks with the delicate reed, and from a sacred oak swarms hum.

---

29. While architectural structures are not very common ways of representing poetry, they occur in Pindar and Callimachus. Appropriately, themes of victory and Callimachean sensibility characterize Vergil's description of the temple (Wilkinson 1969, 168; Thomas 1983, 92-101).

30. Goodfellow (1981, 12-22) surveys the correspondences between Vergil's description and the topography of the region.

31. Wimmel 1960, 228.

32. On bees representing poetry, see Pindar, *Pythian* 10.53-54. On swans as musical birds, see Callimachus, *Hymn* 4.252; Leonidas, *Palatine Anthology* 7.19.2; Aristophanes, *Birds* 870; Euripides, *Iphigeneia in Tauris* 1104; Lucretius, *De Rerum Natura* 3.6-7, 4.181-82; Horace, *Odes* 2.20.1-3, 10-12, 4.2.25; Vergil, *Eclogues* 8.55 and 9.29 (Coleman 1989, *ad Eclogue* 9.29).

The focus in all three cases on the reeds or other plants that grow along the river's banks unites the passages, particularly *Georgics* 3 and *Eclogue* 7, which both contain the phrase *praetexit harundine ripas.*[33] The three passages suggest that Vergil saw the Mincius as a location for poetry, whether metaphors for poet or poem are placed near it. In addition, the Mincius is the river of Vergil's homeland, making it a natural choice for this close link to the poet and his creative process.

As a part of the scene as a whole, the river provides a focal point in the landscape in which author and honorand exist, just as the narrative form is the poetic medium in which Vergil practices his art. Instead of the irrigation ditches of *Eclogue* 3, in *Georgics* 3 the poet governs (*agitabo*, 18) four-horse chariots. The image looks ahead to Octavian's role as *triumphator* (26-36).[34] It also grants the poet a share of that fame: *illi victor ego* (17) artfully links the success of the two and we are perhaps reminded of the Homeric currency of *kleos* that cements the reciprocal relationship between poet and hero.[35] In addition, the combination of chariots driven near a river with a temple recalls the route of triumphal processions through Rome from the Tiber to the Temple of Jupiter Optimus Maximus. Like the river, the evocation of a triumph lends motion to a static monument, which itself represents a triumph. Like a narrative, a triumph arranges images in a sequence and ensures that observers experience them in that order.[36]

Vergil's vision of his future poem as a landscape enables him to give spatial reality to words as yet only potential and to demonstrate the monumental nature of the planned work. The river in this passage functions to more accurately reflect the dynamic nature of poetry than would an architectural analogy on its own. By locating the temple next to the Mincius, Vergil references the theme of poetic inspiration, a concept he elsewhere associates with the river of his native region. Inspiration suggests a new beginning, an idea appropriate to the anticipated epic and to the proem that contains the announcement. In addition, as with

---

33. Mynors explains the distinction between *praetexit harundine ripas* and *herboso flumine*, asserting that although *herboso* could refer to the sort of reeds denoted by *harundine*, it normally indicates grassy banks (1990, *ad Georgics* 2.198-99).

34. Wimmel 1960, 167, 169.

35. More than "fame," *kleos* represents the transmission of heroic glory via the singer to those who hear and learn his song. See Nagy 1974, 245-52 and Segal 1994, 85-88.

36. Quint enumerates the similarities between epic and triumphal processions: "Epic loves a parade, perhaps because the procession that keeps its shape through both space and time resembles its own regular verse schemes—meter, rhyme, stanza—that similarly spacialise time and join the poem's beginning in interconnected sequence to its end" (1993, 31). Versnel places the origin of the triumphal procession in new years' festivals. These processions of the new consuls reinforce the political hierarchy and create an auspicious atmosphere through ordered ritual (1970, 302). Like triumphs, other processions, such as funerals use order as a part of ritual, while also using it to bring remote events before the eyes of an audience. By including masks of ancestors, the procession enacts the past, just as a triumph places before a Roman audience events that occurred in remote locations. Versnel disputes any connection between the origins of the funeral and the triumph and argues that many of the similarities are features of a large group of rituals and, thus, do not indicate any particular link between triumph and funeral (Versnel 1970, 117-22). Nonetheless, the analogous use of ordered processions in these two rituals is helpful in understanding the effect of triumphal tableaus on their audience.

the other passages considered in this section, in the proem to *Georgics* 3, we can discern as separate elements poet and poem. Like the poet of *Eclogue* 3, the poet of the proposed epic envisions authorial control in the form of a charioteer, with the poet as architect of his own poem. Also like *Eclogue* 3, a watercourse imposes structure: in *Eclogue* 3 it imposes an endpoint, in *Georgics* 3 it offers a path, along which the charioteer proceeds.

The Tiber and Prophecy

As Aeneas embarks upon the Italian leg of his journey, he orders a change of course that carries the Trojan ships into the Tiber. At the same time, Vergil opens the second half of his poem, invoking the muse Erato. Everything about Aeneas's approach to the Tiber is auspicious:

> Neptunus uentis impleuit uela secundis,
> atque fugam dedit et praeter uada feruida uexit.
>   Iamque rubescebat radiis mare et aethere ab alto
> Aurora in roseis fulgebat lutea bigis,
> cum uenti posuere omnisque repente resedit
> flatus, et in lento luctantur marmore tonsae.
> atque hic Aeneas ingentem ex aequore lucum
> prospicit. hunc inter fluuio Tiberinus amoeno
> uerticibus rapidis et multa flauus harena
> in mare prorumpit. uariae circumque supraque
> adsuetae ripis uolucres et fluminis alueo
> aethera mulcebant cantu lucoque uolabant.
> flectere iter sociis terraeque aduertere proras
> imperat et laetus fluuio succedit opaco.

> (Vergil, *Aeneid* 7.23-36)

Neptune filled their sails with following winds and granted them their flight and carried them beyond the turbulent shallows.
    And now the sea was growing red with dawn, and from the upper air golden Aurora shone in her rosy chariot, when the winds stilled and every blast at once ceased, and the oars toiled in marble-smooth water. And from the water, Aeneas sees a huge grove. In its midst, the Tiber with its pleasant stream bursts forth into the sea with rapid whirlpools and yellow with much sand. Around and above, many-colored birds, accustomed to the banks and channel of the river, were soothing the air with song and flying through the grove. He commands his men to change the course and to turn the prows to land, and happy he enters the shady stream.

Neptune has provided favorable winds (*ventis . . . secundis*, 23) that subside just in time for Aeneas to notice the Tiber.[37] The river, described as *fluvio Tiberinus*

---

37. This detail is Vergil's innovation. Traditionally, Aeneas's landing was placed south of the Tiber (Williams 1987, *ad Aeneid* 7.25).

amoeno (30), is inviting: the grove of trees, birds, and flowing water complete the *locus amoenus*.[38]

Immediately following the description of this idyllic landscape comes the poet's invocation:

> Nunc age, qui reges, Erato, quae tempora, rerum
> quis Latio antiquo fuerit status, aduena classem
> cum primum Ausoniis exercitus appulit oris,
> expediam, et primae reuocabo exordia pugnae.
> tu uatem, tu, diua, mone. dicam horrida bella,
> dicam acies actosque animis in funera reges,
> Tyrrhenamque manum totamque sub arma coactam
> Hesperiam. maior rerum mihi nascitur ordo,
> maius opus moueo.

(Vergil, Aeneid 7.37-45)

> Come now, Erato, I will set out who were the kings, what was the history of events, how ancient Latium stood, when first the foreign army touched its fleet to Ausonian shores, and I will recall the beginnings of first hostility. You, goddess, advise your bard. I will relate terrible wars, I will tell of battle lines and kings driven to death by passion, I will tell of Tyrrhenian bands, and all Hesperia forced to arms. A greater tale is born for me, I undertake a greater task.

In his appeal to the muse, Vergil takes for himself a role similar to that he has just granted Aeneas. While he invites the muse's presence, the poet himself will control the narrative, as the emphatically placed first-person *expediam* makes clear (40). Likewise, Aeneas himself gives the command to enter the river, although Neptune provides the conditions that make this move possible.

In addition to its role as a point of embarkation both for the next stage of Aeneas's travels and for the second half of the poem, the Tiber provides a course for words and narrative. Rumor travels simultaneously with the Trojans and her report of their arrival has reached the cities of Ausonia by the time Aeneas and his men complete the initial leg of their journey upstream (*Aeneid* 7.104-6). Words have flown while ships were in motion on the river and, as words and ships reach their destinations, there is a tension between idyllic setting and growing unease, similar to that achieved in the invocation. Note the evocation of the Sibyl's prophecy in book 6 (*bella, horrida bella, et Thybrim multo spumantem sanguine cerno, Aeneid* 6.86-87); there the impact of the war on the Italian landscape is envisioned (the Tiber flowing with blood). By juxtaposing an idyllic image of the Tiber with a reminiscence of a particularly horrible picture of it, Vergil not only suggests the price at which Trojan occupation of the Tiber will come, but he also foreshadows the beginning of the war itself, when an idyllic river scene will turn to bloodshed as Ascanius shoots Silvia's pet stag (*Aeneid* 7.493-99), the news of which will be reported by Allecto and will travel from one Italian body of water to another (from Lake Trivia to the

---

38. See Curtius 1953, 195-200 on the essential components of a *locus amoenus*.

River Nar to Lake Velinus, 7.516-17). Indeed, the first two Italian victims of the war, Almo and Galaesus are named for Italian rivers (7.531-39).

So we see in *Aeneid* 7 rivers supporting travel not only of Vergil's characters, but also of information. In a number of instances they mark important moments in the arrival of war in Italy. The parallels between Aeneas's embarkation on a river journey and Vergil's own embarkation on the second half of his epic suggest that we see the river as a conveyer of the narrative itself.

In *Aeneid* 8, travel on the Tiber begins again. We first see Aeneas troubled, his mind rushing here and there as if carried on turbulent water:[39] First Vergil uses a metaphor (*magno curarum fluctuat aestu*, 19) and then a simile comparing Aeneas's mind to light that dances as it is reflected on water (22-25). Despite the restlessness of his mind, Aeneas finally lies still, asleep on the riverbank, until Tiberinus appears to him in a dream and spurs him to action. At this point we are brought back to Aeneas's arrival at the Tiber in *Aeneid* 7:

> prospicit. hunc inter fluvio Tiberinus amoeno
>
> (Vergil, *Aeneid* 7.30)[40]

> huic deus ipse loci fluvio Tiberinus amoeno
>
> (Vergil, *Aeneid* 8.31)

> . . . the very god of the place, Tiberinus with his pleasant stream . . .

Seeing the god Tiberinus for the first time replicates seeing the river for the first time and so we are reminded of embarking upon a river journey and a narrative simultaneously.[41]

In fact, Tiberinus himself speaks to Aeneas. The type of speech he employs, prophecy, is closely linked to Vergil's role as author. Both prophet and author mediate the course of the story. The prophecy itself, however, draws attention to the distinction between river and river god. There is a disparity between the prophecy and its fulfillment. While the god Tiberinus promises in his prophecy to guide the ships upstream so that the rowers will be able to overcome the current, the river fulfills the prediction by staying its current so that there is no struggle against the current at all:

> ipse ego te ripis et recto flumine ducam,
> adversum remis superes subvectus ut amnem.
>
> (Vergil, *Aeneid* 8.57-58)

> I myself will lead you along the banks and straight upstream, so that, carried by your oars, you may overcome the opposing current.

---

39. Simile based on Lucretius, *De Rerum Natura* 4.211-13 and Apollonius Rhodius, *Argonautica* 3.744-60.

40. (And from the water, Aeneas) sees (a huge grove.) In its midst, the Tiber with its pleasant stream (bursts forth into the sea with rapid whirlpools and yellow with much sand.)

41. On the journey itself, see ch. 7.

Thybris ea fluvium, quam longa est, nocte tumentem
leniit, et tacita refluens ita substitit unda,
mitis ut in morem stagni placidaeque paludis
sterneret aequor aquis, remo ut luctamen abesset.
ergo iter inceptum celerant rumore secundo

(Vergil, Aeneid 8.86-90)

During the whole length of that night, the Tiber calmed his swelling stream,
and flowing back with silent wave thus stood still, so that in the manner of a
calm pool or unruffled marsh he smoothed his expanse with his waters, so that
struggle might not touch the oars. Therefore the men speed the initiated voyage
with encouraging shouts.

The differences between god and element perhaps account for the two strategies
for aiding the Trojans' progress. The god envisions for himself a directive role,
whereas the river can alter its behavior but only interact with the Trojans in a
limited way. That the strategies of god and river are just two sides of the same
coin is evident from the language in the two passages. In the prophecy, the Tiber's stream is *adversum* and must be overcome (58). In the fulfillment, struggle
is absent and rather than meeting any opposition the Trojans are aided by *rumore secundo* (90).[42] While the god claimed that he (*ipse ego*, 57) would provide
help, in fact words give the impetus (*rumore*, 90). The shifting roles of god,
river, and words demonstrate the overlapping functions these entities can have.
In both prophecy and fulfillment, it is a combination of river and speech that
enables the Trojans to navigate the Tiber. Parallels can be drawn between poet
and river god. Parallels also exist between poem and river, as will be clear when
we return to this passage in chapter 7.

Ovid and the Achelous

Like the Tiber, the Achelous in Ovid's *Metamorphoses* speaks in a way that
suggests the role of the poet. In *Metamorphoses* 8, the Achelous in flood effectively holds up Theseus's return to Athens (*Metamorphoses* 8.547-59). While it
is the excessive water of the river in flood that initially stops the hero's progress,
the river god has a parallel function, as he detains Theseus's party by telling
stories. In this episode, Ovid frequently plays on the dual identity of Achelous as
water and god, thus encouraging readers to see them working in tandem. As
Achelous introduces himself, water seamlessly becomes god (*fecitque moras
Achelous eunti / imbre tumens: "succede meis," ait "inclite, tectis,"* 550-51).

---

42. This disparity between prophecy and fulfillment reverses the discrepancy that occurs between the Sibyl's prediction and the plucking of the golden bough in *Aeneid* 6. There, the Sibyl
implies that Aeneas will pluck the golden bough easily, but, when he comes to pull the bough from
the tree, Aeneas detaches it only with difficulty. In *Aeneid* 8, Tiberinus implies that the Trojans will
be able to travel upstream, but laboriously. As it turns out, the obstacle is removed completely.

Ovid then accentuates the distinction he had elided by having Achelous refer to his own waters (*nec te committe rapacibus undis*, 551).[43]

Like the god emerging from his stream, words that could apply to narrative as well as river appear in the description of the flood. The verb *volvere* (552) can represent the unrolling of a book roll as well as the current of a river.[44] The type of narrative referenced by a river in flood also is implied. Achelous describes the flood subsiding by saying *dum tenues capiat suus alveus undas* (559). The poetically loaded term *tenuis* recalls Callimachean ideals and the specific formulation that poetry can be a wide river or a small spring. By suggesting that this quality characterizes the end of the flood, Ovid implies that Achelous's narrative will be on a grand scale. Indeed it occupies the remainder of the book and culminates with a tale about Hercules; it begins with a description of a banquet and ends with a battle scene.

Also like a river in flood, the narrative cannot be contained: it flows over the book boundary into *Metamorphoses* 9, where the action resumes without missing a beat.[45] We soon learn that Achelous's tale has lasted all night (*Metamorphoses* 9.89-94). Dawn finds neither narrative nor flood at an end, but it affords Theseus and his companions an opportunity to depart:

> discedunt iuvenes, neque enim dum flumina pacem
> et placidos habeant lapsus totaeque residant
> opperiuntur aquae. vultus Achelous agrestes
> et lacerum cornu mediis caput abdidit undis.
>
> (Ovid, *Metamorphoses* 9.94-97)

> The young men depart, for they do not wait until the streams have peace and quiet flowings and all the waters subside. Achelous hid his rustic features and his head, wounded as to his horn, in the middle of the waves.

The flood continues, but, without an audience, the narrator Achelous disappears into the waters from which he emerged in 8.550-51. This event, however, is, like the death of Orpheus, an equivocal ending.[46] The tales of Hercules continue without Achelous as narrator or character, as if, like a river in flood, the topic must run its course.

Ovid exploits the parallelism between river and god and river and narrative to a humorous end. Both Achelous and his river serve the same purpose in the narrative: they delay the hero. Theseus's response to the flood, leaving before it subsides, is identical to the response one might expect of someone faced with a

---

43. As Anderson notes, Ovid is fond of suggesting "the fun a sophisticated person can have with the anthropomorphic concepts of mythology" (1972, *ad* 8.550; see also his comments on lines 556 and 583).

44. We see a similar situation in the tale of Byblis: her name evokes books, the written word precipitates her ruin, and she finally turns into flowing water (Ovid, *Metamorphoses* 9.450-665). On *volvo*, see ch. 4, "Rivers and Authorial Mediation in the *Eclogues* and *Georgics*."

45. *Metamorphoses* 8 ends with Achelous groaning over the loss of his horn and the next book begins with Theseus asking the river god why he groans.

46. On the death of Orpheus, see Vergil, *Georgics* 4.453-527.

lengthy narrative: he finally departs while the story goes on. That the poet's own voice takes over the narrative when the river god relinquishes his role as story-teller suggests the primacy of the tale and its status as the driving force in the poem. That the poet steps so easily into Achelous's role perhaps suggests Ovid's acknowledgment that his poem is lengthy and filled with tales that end by prompting additional stories.

Whether it inspires, acts as a metaphor or functions as a character, flowing water has an essential connection to words. In all of these contexts we see the self-referential possibilities afforded poets by rivers. For Vergil, water represents poetic voice in all of his works, often in the context of embarking on or concluding poetic speech. That reference to rivers marks these critical moments in the creative process demonstrates the centrality of rivers to the poet's portrayal of his relationship to his composition.

Chapter Five

Round Rivers: Okeanos and Bounded Narrative

By virtue of its round shape, the river Okeanos encompasses everything but confounds beginnings and endings. This unusual property makes Okeanos a useful metaphor. The shield of Achilles in the *Iliad* is an early example of the symbolic possibilities Okeanos holds. The idea of Okeanos as the ultimate boundary of the world, however, has long been questioned. Herodotus rejects the neatly finite picture of a world bounded by Okeanos. As we shall see, Vergil explores the intersection of these traditions in his description of the shield of Aeneas.

The Shield of Aeneas and Okeanos

Much of this section will focus on a river we do not see, namely Okeanos on the shield of Aeneas in *Aeneid* 8. The absence of this river from the shield may seem surprising, given the geographical theme of the shield's central scene and the precedent set by Homer's shield of Achilles. But, in fact, Vergil's exclusion of Okeanos elucidates the principles on which the poet configures his shield. Nonetheless, Vergil has Homer in mind and, as we shall see, Okeanos is an implicit feature of Aeneas's shield.

The shield of Achilles in the *Iliad* possesses some qualities of a map. The description of Okeanos encircling the rim of the shield (*Iliad* 18.606-7) recalls an early Greek worldview in which Okeanos borders the world.[1] In addition, the cosmological entities portrayed in the center of the shield contribute to a reading of the shield as a representation of the entire world (*Iliad* 18.483-89).[2] Between the center and the border of the shield are scenes, probably arranged in concentric circles, emblematic of the world and of human society. These scenes have three basic themes: city life (18.490-540), country life (18.541-89), and the

---

1. Romm 1992, 13-14.

2. The consensus seems to be that the depictions of earth, sky, sun, moon, and constellations are in the center of the shield (Willcock 1978, *ad* 478-608; Taplin 1998, 100; Hubbard 1992, 29, Redfield 1975, 187). Presumably, these would be personifications, while Okeanos would be represented as a river, since it functions as a border.

dance (18.590-605). The depiction of city life shows the city at peace, as evidenced by a marriage and the enactment of justice, and the city at war, as evidenced by a siege and battle. The description of country life follows the cycle of the seasons. The portrayal of a dance echoes the marriage scene and, thus, returns to the images of peace and prosperity with which the human scenes of the shield began.[3]

The cosmic symbols in the shield's center and Okeanos on its rim cast the intervening scenes in a spatial context and imply that these individual vignettes are emblematic of the world as a whole and that the shield is exhaustive in its portrayal of the human condition. By endowing the shield of Achilles with characteristics of a map, Homer creates various levels of representation. Okeanos forms the outermost rim of the shield and also marks the ultimate boundary of the world. In addition, the description of Okeanos concludes the poetic description of the shield, thus functioning as a boundary within the poem. In linking the endpoints of object, world, and description, Homer projects a physical structure onto verbal art. Indeed, the quality of roundness, just as essential to Okeanos as its identity as a boundary, also applies to all three levels of the shield passage: Okeanos runs around the edge of the earth and around the rim of the shield. It also participates in the ring composition of the shield passage by balancing the mention of the sea in the description of cosmic forces at the beginning of the shield passage. In this way, the description of the shield, like the world itself, is framed by cosmic forces. The description begins with earth, sky, sea (θάλασσαν, 18.483), sun, and moon. A listing of selected constellations includes a mention of Okeanos (the observation that the great bear does not bathe in Okeanos, 18.489). The reference to the sea perhaps evokes the notion of primordial water (see above, pp. 8-14), another aspect of Okeanos. The mention of Okeanos itself is, like the description of Okeanos flowing around the border of the shield, an expression of a boundary or limit. Here we see Homer endow a river with significance as part of the world, part of an object depicting that world, and part of poetry that describes that object.[4]

The three interpretive levels found in Homer's description of the shield of Achilles—object, map, and poetic creation—also figure in Vergil's description of the shield of Aeneas. The description begins with a summary of the shield's images: the scenes are prophetic and tell the story of Italy and of Roman victories (*Aeneid* 8.626-29). Vergil first describes scenes relating to Rome's founding: the descendents of Ascanius, Romulus and Remus suckled by the she-wolf, and the rape of the Sabine women (*Aeneid* 8.629-38). Next Vergil describes the scenes located at the top of the shield: Manlius defending the Capitol against the Gauls and the Salian priests with their shields that fell from the sky (*Aeneid* 8.639-66). The next scenes described are located at the bottom of the shield and, appropriately, involve the underworld. As Capitoline and sky contrast with un-

---

3. See Taplin 1998, 100-106.
4. Hubbard discusses the relationship between poet and craftsman, poetry and artifact (1992, 27, 34).

derworld, so Manlius's heroism contrasts with Catiline's crimes. The underworld, however, also contains images of Roman pietas, as Cato dispenses laws to the righteous (*Aeneid* 8.666-70).

A border separates the visual catalogue of Roman historical highlights from the central scene (*Aeneid* 8.671-74). It consists of the sea with dolphins swimming in it, and, while it may echo Okeanos bordering the shield of Achilles, this sea serves as an internal border, perhaps separating all of the preceding scenes from one another.[5] The description of the border itself separates the elaborate description of the central scene from the more concise treatments of the other episodes from Roman history. In this sense as well, the border is an internal boundary. The word *inter* (8.671) emphasizes the difference between this boundary and Okeanos: the *mare* on Aeneas's shield has scenes on both sides of it. In some ways, Vergil's sea has more in common with the harbor described in the Hesiodic *Shield of Herakles* than with Homer's Okeanos. Both Hesiod and Vergil depict dolphins in the sea and both descriptions come near the middle of the two ecphrases.[6]

The explicitly geographical portion of Vergil's shield is the central scene. In addition to the Battle of Actium, the scene seems to reflect, at least indirectly, Octavian's triple triumph.[7] As such, it depicts the Roman conquest of the world and the resulting expansion of borders. But the extension of the Roman Empire to the edges of the earth involves no reference to Okeanos. Rather, Vergil names several remote rivers lying in the East and North.[8] This way of referring to the edges of the earth recalls the Herodotean view of the world more than the Homeric.[9]

By updating his image of the world, Vergil replaces Homeric imagination with ethnographic theory. The center of the shield, appropriately enough, represents the center of the *oikoumene*: the Mediterranean region. Egypt is in opposition to Rome, both as a foe and as geographical and ethnographical opposite (*Aeneid* 8.711-19).

While Okeanos concludes the description of the shield of Achilles by evoking legends of the ends of the earth, real rivers end Vergil's account of the shield of Aeneas. By replacing the Homeric ending with an ethnographic one,

---

5. Williams 1987, *ad* 8.671.

6. Hesiod, *Shield of Herakles* 208-11. The lines referring to dolphins may be an interpolation, however (Russo 1965, *ad* 209-11).

7. Östenberg argues that although the procession does not precisely describe the victories celebrated by the Triple Triumph of 29 BC, it does reflect the purpose of those triumphs: to advertise Octavian's conquest of the entire world (1999, 156-57). Gurval suggests that the triumphal scene on the shield projects Augustan victory beyond Actium and the Triple Triumph by including images such as Nomads, Gelonians, the Araxes river, and the Temple of Apollo on the Palatine that would not have appeared in the Triple Triumph (1998, 35).

8. The Euphrates represents the western Asia Minor, the Rhine northern Europe, and the Araxes the Caspian Sea region (Östenberg 1999, 157). The locations are mentioned in order of increasing distance from Italy.

9. Herodotus takes issue with the Homeric view of the world as a disc surrounded by Okeanos (*History* 2.23, 4.8, 4.36), preferring to envision a boundless expanse extending in all directions beyond the known world (*History* 3.98, 4.17, 4.185, 5.9). See Nagy 1990, 98; Romm 1992, 33-38.

Vergil shows how the Romans have moved beyond imagining the edges of the earth and now touch them with their empire. In this way, the past gives way to the present, just as the scenes from Rome's earlier days cede pride of place to images of Actium and empire.

Vergil's description of the rivers themselves evokes ethnographical writing. In addition to using the names of local peoples or rivers to refer to geographical regions, Vergil provides descriptive details consistent with the methods of ethnographers.[10] The rivers mentioned each have an individual character that resembles the character of the region's inhabitants. On the shield we find three rivers, each associated with one or more groups of foreign peoples. This tripartite structure reinforces the interpretation of the passage as a reflection of Octavian's triple triumph. We first have a list of conquered peoples, who march in a docile procession although they are still armed (*Aeneid* 8.722-26), paired with the Euphrates, which is said to flow *iam mollior undis* (726).[11] Although not all of the peoples mentioned live in the region of the Euphrates, they seem to give a kind of overview of conquered peoples in the same way the description of the Euphrates seems to represent most prominently the contrast between past violence and present submission embodied in a triumph.

The remaining two rivers on the shield are paired more closely with peoples of their regions. The Rhine is associated with the Morini, who receive the epithet *extremi hominum* (*Aeneid* 8.727). Servius elaborates saying that the Morini live close to Okeanos. The Rhine, too, was envisioned by some as emptying into Okeanos.[12] Perhaps the clearest example of characteristics shared between a river and a people is the final pairing we see on the shield. The Dahae, referred to as *indomiti* (*Aeneid* 8.728), are linked to the Araxes, dubbed *indignatus*. Both epithets, identical in their first three letters, immediately precede the names they modify and both reference the recalcitrant nature apparently indigenous to the region.

This depiction of the world according to ethnographic principles may be one reason Aeneas does not understand the shield. In addition to revealing future events that are beyond Aeneas's ken, the shield contains a postheroic age view of the world. It is an artifact from the future, which both contains prophecies and is a prophecy. Aeneas understands neither the content of the images nor the visual idiom employed. A familiar reference point, Okeanos as a boundary of the earth, has been replaced with unfamiliar geographical features and a perhaps disorienting lack of a definite edge. In addition, the edges of the earth do not coincide with the rim of the shield: the scenes that focus on the city of Rome are

---

10. Cf. the Hippocratic belief that the waters of all places were unique and that the characteristics of local water influenced the health of inhabitants (*Airs, Waters, Places* 1, 7).

11. The river's change in current mirrors the newly tamed inhabitants of the region. Although here the river's former character is alluded to only by the comparative *mollior*, perhaps Vergil directs readers to Callimachus, *Hymn* 2.108 for an image of the Euphrates as a river with a powerful current (Ἀσσυρίου ποταμοῖο μέγας ῥόος). On Vergil's allusion to Callimachus in this line, see Scodel and Thomas 1984, 339.

12. Romm 1992, 147.

arranged around the edges of the scene that depicts the most distant parts of the world. In this way, Vergil challenges the Homeric notion that a shield provides the appropriate shape for a map and that the earth possesses a round edge bounded by Okeanos.

In fact, surveying occurrences of *Oceanus* in the *Aeneid* reveals that Okeanos as a structuring principle is a mark of the heroic age, as opposed to the Roman future. References to Okeanos as a structuring principle of the world are part of the contemporary idiom of Aeneas's time. Of the nine references to Okeanos in the *Aeneid*, four refer to the edges of the earth[13] and five tell the time of day or the season.[14] The latter group implies that Okeanos constitutes the edge of the world, as the references to time depend on the belief that sun and stars set into and rise from Okeanos. All but two of the references to Okeanos involve the contemporary world of the *Aeneid*'s characters. Two mentions of Okeanos occur in prophecies that foresee the Roman empire extending to the shores of Okeanos (*Aeneid* 1.287, 7.101). While these prophecies delivered in words involve Okeanos, prophetic material that involves visual evidence of future events presents an image of the world appropriate to the time at which the predicted events will occur. The shield is one instance and the parade of future Romans Aeneas sees in the underworld is the other (*Aeneid* 6.785-88). There too, Augustus's empire is described as extending to various remote locales as Aeneas is allowed to gaze upon the Roman future.[15]

The shield as an artifact presents the world understood ethnographically, apparently because it uses an idiom consistent with the time it depicts. This departure from Homer in the visual realm, however, means that there is no Okeanos to provide a neat conclusion to the description, demarcating it from the surrounding narrative just as on the shield of Achilles, Okeanos flowing around the rim of the shield provides a border for the object. Vergil's foreign rivers suggest the Herodotean map: a world that goes on indefinitely beyond what has been explored as of yet. Vergil's ecphrasis has a definite structure, however: one that is dependent both on Homer and on Okeanos.

It has been noted that Vergil changes the sequence of events in narrating the hero's acquisition of his new shield. Gransden observes that the delivery of the shield comes before its description in Vergil so that the reader's view of the

---

13. In *Aeneid* 1.287, Jupiter assures Venus that a Trojan Caesar will be descended from Aeneas and will have Okeanos as the boundary of his empire; in *Aeneid* 4.480 Dido claims she has a spell from Ethiopia near the bounds of Okeanos; in *Aeneid* 7.101 Latinus receives a prophecy that a foreign son-in-law will guarantee his descendants an empire wherever the sun looks on both sides of Okeanos; in *Aeneid* 7.226 Ilioneus explains to Latinus that the Trojan War is known even to those Okeanos keeps far away.

14. In *Aeneid* 1.745 Iopas sings why the winter suns rush to Okeanos; in *Aeneid* 2.250 as the Trojans sleep their last night in Troy, night hurries from Okeanos; in *Aeneid* 4.129 as Juno plans the wedding for Aeneas and Dido, Aurora leaves Okeanos; in *Aeneid* 8.589 Pallas is like the morning star bathed in Okeanos lifting up his head and dissolving the darkness; in *Aeneid* 11.1 Aurora leaves Okeanos.

15. Incidentally, these passages contain the only two occurrences of the title "Augustus" in the *Aeneid* (Gransden 1976, *ad Aeneid* 8.678).

shield is mediated through Aeneas's viewing of it rather than the divine crafting of the object, as in Homer.[16] Vergil's rearrangement is not a displacement, however. In Vergil's reworking, the key elements of Homer's narrative all remain in the same place relative to their neighbors. It is as if Vergil imagined the beginning and end of the Homeric narrative joined to form a circle, which could then be entered at any point and traveled around in either direction. This is, of course, the essential characteristic of Okeanos: a watercourse that, instead of having a linear structure that may divide things on one side from those on the other, flows in a circle, confounding beginning and end while containing all within its course.

The *Iliad* and *Aeneid* passages are structured as shown in table 5.1:

Table 5.1: Structure of the Shield Passages in Homer and Vergil

Iliad 18	*Aeneid* 8
1. Thetis promises Achilles new armor (134).	3. Venus visits Vulcan; asks for armor (382).
2. (Interlude with events not related to shield)	2. (Interlude with events not related to shield)
3. Thetis visits Hephaistos; asks for armor (368).	1. Aeneas explains unusual heavenly phenomena as armor promised by Venus (530). (Interlude with events not related to shield)
4. Shield is described from center to rim (478).	6. Venus appears in sky with arms (608).
5. Other pieces of armor are described (609).	5. Other pieces of armor are described (619).
6. Thetis, like a hawk, brings Achilles armor (614).	4. Shield is described from rim to center (626).

With the exception of one additional pause in Vergil's description of the production and delivery of the arms, the two narratives contain the same elements.[17] The way in which Vergil changes the order makes a circular structure of Homer's narrative. Vergil begins his account at neither the beginning nor the end of Homer's. In fact, the beginning and end of Homer's narrative form the center of Vergil's description. Nevertheless, each of the numbered elements in the *Iliad* passage retains its position relative to the others when they make their reappearance in *Aeneid* 8. This is precisely the way in which one navigates Okeanos: from any starting point, travel in either direction will result in a return to the starting point. Through this structure of words, then, Vergil emulates the

---

16. Gransden 1976, *ad Aeneid* 8.626-728.

17. This additional pause comes at the center of Vergil's description and at the point at which Homer's beginning and end are brought together, in effect bridging the gap between them.

physical structure of the Homeric shield. The narrative itself provides the all-encompassing circularity we are missing with the lack of Okeanos, while also linking the shield of Aeneas with the shield of Achilles by using Achilles's shield as structure not for images but for words.

The Perils of Circumnavigation

The updated geography of Vergil's shield ecphrasis has Alexandrian as well as Homeric and ethnographical antecedents. In the *Argonautica*, Apollonius Rhodius challenges the idea of a bounded earth, questioning the relevance of the Homeric image of the world for his poem. As in the *Aeneid*, the new worldview involves a futuristic object. In the *Argonautica*, the visual prophecy takes the form of an actual map as opposed to a shield that shares key aspects of a map.[18] As a real navigational aid, the map in the *Argonautica* helps to guide the heroes on their journey, rather than functioning passively as the object of marvel.

The essential feature of Apollonius's map is its river. In *Argonautica* 4, Jason and his men learn from their visit to Aea that a river, the Ister, is the key to their homeward journey (4.277-93). This rivercentric view of geography should not surprise, given that the Aeans originally hail from Egypt. For them, the Ister recreates the Nile's role as a geographical marker and essential tool for survival.[19] Indeed, an account of the colonists' origins immediately precedes the description of the map, an object that is in its own right the product of knowledge gained in the course of their transplantation (4.279-81). The description of the Nile emphasizes the river's antiquity and its life-giving force (4.263-71). Apollonius also communicates the Nile's primacy when he describes the river's role in irrigation: it takes the place of rain, which, as Apollonius notes, comes from Zeus himself. By fulfilling a function of the king of the gods, the river takes for itself the leading role in its landscape. Likewise, the Ister is the focal point of the map created by Egyptian explorers who settled Aea. Like the Nile, the Ister offers a benefit to those who understand its nature: it can return travelers safely to the Mediterranean.

In addition to being an alternative to the Nile, the Ister is an alternative to Okeanos. It provides an inland route by which the Argonauts will achieve the same destination to which the curved course of Okeanos would have taken them. To emphasize this idea, Apollonius employs ring composition when describing the Argonauts' passage along the Ister (*Argonautica* 4.305-8, 313-14).[20]

The purpose of the map is to illustrate the advantages of an inland journey via a river over a circumnavigation via Okeanos. The Argonauts' actual trip, while it follows this map in its course along the Ister, later fails to follow the principle of this map (that an inland journey via rivers is preferable to a circumnavigation via Okeanos). The Argonauts must again be redirected lest they suc-

---

18. On the artifact as a map, see Clare 2002, 129-30.
19. Cf. Greek colonists who cast new rivers in old roles in Magna Graecia (see above, ch. 3).
20. Williams 1991, 125.

cumb to the perils of Okeanos (*Argonautica* 4.636-44). Several specific links between the two episodes suggest viewing them as a pair. In addition to their adherence to the principle that inland travel replaces ventures into Okeanos, the recommended routes involve a branching river or a network of interconnected rivers linking two seas or a sea and Okeanos in a way that provides a shortcut for the Argonauts. Finally, in both cases, signs from Hera direct the Argonauts. These signs are complementary: first, as the Argonauts embark on their course up the Ister, Hera gives a visual sign (a trail of light, 4.296-97) that points ahead to the path the Argo should follow. In the second instance, rather than pointing ahead, Hera turns the Argonauts back from an erroneous course, this time with a terrifying cry (4.640-42), an auditory rather than a visual cue.

Several verbal similarities also unite the two passages. When describing the mouths of the Ister and the system of rivers involving the Eridanus, Rhine, and Rhône, Apollonius echoes wording and meter:

ἔνθα διχῇ, τὸ μὲν ἔνθα μεθ᾽ ἡμετέρην²¹ ἅλα βάλλει

Ὠκεανοῦ, τῇ δ᾽ αὖτε μετ᾽ Ἰονίην ἅλα βάλλει

(Apollonius Rhodius, *Argonautica* 4.289, 4.632)

. . . there it divides, on one side it flows out into our sea . . .

(On one side it bursts forth on the shores) of Okeanos, on the other, it flows out into the Ionian Sea.

The metrically equivalent ἡμετέρην and Ἰονίην were similar enough to cause a variant reading of Ἰονίην in 4.289, where it makes no geographical sense, as the Ionian Gulf and the gulf extending upwards from the Trinacrian Sea denote the same body of water, rather than two seas connected by the Ister. Although Apollonius clearly did not intend the two lines to reference the same body of water, the echo calls attention to the repetition of a geographical and narrative pattern.

As the Argonauts are about to mistakenly enter Okeanos via the Rhine (*Argonautica* 4.637-38), Apollonius describes the Rhine as emptying into a gulf of Okeanos (κόλπον ἐς Ὠκεανοῦ, 4.638). With Hera's intervention, they reverse direction before reaching this gulf. The Ister, too, was described as emptying into a gulf (τὸ δ᾽ ὄπισθε βαθὺν διὰ κόλπον ἵησιν / σχιζόμενος πόντου Τρινακρίου εἰσανέχοντα, 4.290-91). In their previous river journey, when the Argonauts exited the Ister into the Ionian Gulf, the Colchians forced them to backtrack (4.294-337). It was this retracing of their steps in the Ionian Gulf that occasioned their entry into the Eridanus/Rhine/Rhône system of rivers. The point at which Rhine meets Okeanos is called a gulf only in the context of the Argo-

---

21. Wilamowitz's conjecture. Other conjectures include ἠοίην (Platt) and ἠῴην (Gerhard). All of these would refer to the Black Sea and thus be consistent with the idea of the Ister connecting the region of Colchis with the region of Jason's home. The manuscripts read Ἰονίην.

nauts' backtracking. Earlier in the passage, Apollonius referred to the mouth of the Rhine as the beach of Okeanos (ἀκτάς / 'Ωκεανοῦ, 4.631-32).

Hera's signs also receive similar descriptions. In both passages, Hera sends a portent originating in the sky (οὐρανίης, 4.297; οὐρανόθεν, 4.641) and emanating outward from there (ἐπιπρό, 4.296; προθοῦσα, 4.641). Whether visual or auditory, the signs are conceived in terms of their origin and destination. Apollonius emphasizes the protective interest Hera takes in the Argonauts as she continues to help them even when the task becomes repetitive.

It has been noted that Apollonius's redirection of the Argonauts at the confluence of the Eridanus and the Rhône has metatextual significance. Romm notes Apollonius's emphatic refusal to send the Argonauts on an *exokeanismos*, a route that would follow Homeric patterns both narrative and geographical. Romm sees this departure on Apollonius's part as a sign of the poet's intent not to venture into the kind of poetry that Alexandrian sensibilities associated with Okeanos.[22] In addition, the repetition of the motif of the redirected journey emphasizes its symbolic meaning. As a prophetic object, the map shows the same triple significance as the Homeric and Vergilian shields. On the level of physical object: the map is a recording of a prior voyage, one made by the ancestors of the map's owners. Those who currently possess the map reuse it to direct a subsequent journey that is a return rather than an outbound trip to a new homeland. On the level of the plot: the Argonauts must from time to time retrace their steps in their attempt to make progress toward their home.[23] On the level of the poem: Apollonius is revisiting a tradition others have treated, but his narrative often forges a new path through the material. With the paired episodes of redirection, Apollonius intratextually revisits a theme, thus retracing his own steps in creating a pair of scenes that have his characters facing the same dilemma in two distinct textual and geographical locations.

For all his avoidance of Okeanos, Apollonius still manages a kind of circularity in his narrative. In a sense, retracing one's steps is tantamount to going in a circle, so retracing steps and returning to a motif both evoke a circular path, as does the idea of a return trip that takes a route different from the outward journey but still arrives back at the starting point. In addition, the two inland river journeys in *Argonautica* 4 resemble a circular journey in one other way: because of the branching courses of the rivers involved, the Argonauts travel upstream for the first half of their trip along the Ister or Eridanus and then downstream for the second half after reaching the branching point of the Ister or the common source of the Eridanus and Rhône.[24]

Apollonius, then, must follow his Alexandrian map in constructing the Argonauts' voyage. The paired river journeys both reference Homeric geography

---

22. Romm 1992, 195-96. Apollonius's insistence on the fatality of travel via Okeanos contradicts prior accounts of the Argonauts' journey (Green 1997, *ad Argonautica* 4.629-44). This direct refusal of the tradition suggests that change serves some purpose and that it may have metatextual significance.

23. E.g. in the Ionian Gulf and when they head toward Okeanos.

24. Green's translation includes helpful maps (1997, 448-58).

and assert Apollonius's independence from it. Beyond that, however, the river journeys reinforce the cyclical and iterative nature of the Argonauts' trip and of his own poetry. Clare notes the equal focus at the end of the poem on characters and author, as well as the attention called to the fact that the labors of both are coextensive. Text and trip end at the same moment (εἰσαπέβητε, *Argonautica* 4.1781). As for the poet's own journey, the emphasis is on its renewal, rather than on its conclusion. Even before the end of the poem, Apollonius is looking to its afterlife (*Argonautica* 4.1773-74). Although the Argonauts complete their journey, the anticipated repetition of the poem will insure that they retrace their steps again and again.

Likewise, the *Aeneid* suggests a voyage that invites repetition, if we recognize in the last lines of the poem an evocation of its opening. The *Aeneid*'s structure evokes ring composition: the poem begins with *arma virumque* and returns at the end of book 12 to arms and the man. Aeneas acts as a soldier, killing Turnus with his sword, but in response to something that affects him deeply as a human being, the death of Pallas. This dichotomy is Aeneas's essential struggle: how to reconcile the soldier with the man. Like the Argonauts' voyage, Aeneas's trip begins anew every time the poem is read. By evoking the beginning at the end, Vergil perhaps signals that, unlike the *Argonautica*, the final line of *Aeneid* 12 is not the end of Aeneas's journey.

A round river expresses both the finite and the infinite. It provides a boundary for the world, while at the same time offering an endless journey. The only ending is at the starting point, which can serve as a new beginning as well. A round river confounds the characteristic linearity of rivers, just as ring composition invites readers to look back in a narrative rather than always forward. Instead of connecting point A with point B, the round river connects point A with point A, turning forward motion into everlasting iteration. As we have seen, this paradoxical nature of round rivers lends itself to the self-referential context. The progress of a literary work may exploit a round river's infinite iteration, or it may seek to break the pattern and revise its worldview. Repetition, however, is essential to the continued existence of a literary work: it lives on only as long as it is begun again and again.[25]

---

25. For the reception of round rivers, see ch. 8.

Chapter Six

Agmen Aquarum: River Catalogues

While the concept of the round river, Okeanos, represents unity, river catalogues emphasize variety. Underlying this contrast, however, is a similarity in function. Like a river that encircles the whole world, a list of many rivers gives the impression of geographical exhaustiveness. Completeness frequently is a motivating force behind lists. Livy's catalogue of Alban kings represents temporal continuity by filling the gap of years between Aeneas and Romulus, the central figures in the narrative. Livy inserts other figures into the catalogue not to introduce recurring characters, but to bring some continuity to a narrative that draws on several distinct legends.[1]

Likewise, in *Metamorphoses* 1.568-87, Ovid catalogues a number of rivers as a transition from the tale of Apollo and Daphne to that of Jupiter and Io.[2] In that instance, Ovid first mentions the location of the Peneus, bringing back to readers' attention the river he had introduced as Daphne's father. In this location, other river gods gather to comfort Peneus for his loss. These rivers do not play a role in the next phase of the narrative, but create a sense of geographical completeness—Ovid even adds to his brief catalogue a statement that all the rivers soon joined them—which the next lines immediately undercut. Despite the illusion that the rivers of Greece have gathered, the most important river for the narrative is the one that is missing. Ovid calls our attention to the absence of Inachus, the reason for which consists of the events of the next episode: his daughter Io is missing, and we learn in a flashback the fate she has met. The rivers in Ovid's list also foreshadow the spatial concerns that resurface in the tale of Io. Just as the mention of numerous rivers of Greece suggests a tour of the area, Ovid's description of Io's wanderings calls attention to geographical variety. Indeed, she ends her journey at the Nile, a unique and exotic river.[3]

Vergil employs river catalogues as much to interact with the literary past as with the setting he has created. This intersection of poetic and physical geogra-

---

1. See Ogilvie 1965, *ad* Livy, *Ab Urbe Condita* 1.3.6.

2. Bernhard 1986, 323.

3. See Herodotus, *History* 2.19. There, Herodotus mentions that the Nile has a certain property that is the opposite of every other river. As such, it is an appropriate location for the reversal of Io's metamorphosis.

phies characterizes the world Vergil's characters inhabit. In this way, Vergil's catalogues (like rivers themselves) serve a temporal purpose: his settings encompass poetic time.

Lists as Verbal Maps

As catalogues, lists of rivers frequently provide continuity in a narrative, specifically geographical continuity. In addition, they may signify motion and provide links to the outer frame of the narrative.[4] In addition to the obvious criterion that they contain a number of names, river catalogues display other features that define catalogues. Epithets are common, as well as the repetition of "and." The names have an effect through their sound as well as their meaning, often evoking foreign locales.[5]

River catalogues are a species of geographical catalogues, which usually present a kind of narrative map, providing not only the information that a map gives, but also putting forth a "reading" of the map. The author may direct readers to the features worthy of notice and, in addition, control the order in which those features are experienced. In this way, the catalogue of ships in *Iliad* 2 suggests a map. The catalogue of women in *Odyssey* 11 also presents its entries in order from north to south, perhaps, as Northrup suggests, both as a mnemonic and as a reflection of Odysseus's "spatial return to his own country."[6] *Periploi* serve a similar function in a technical genre. They create verbal maps through catalogue by mentioning places in a logical order, specifically the order in which those places are encountered on a coastal voyage.[7]

Poetic catalogues of rivers may not be arranged geographically, but, instead, may reflect other principles with their structure. This structure frequently indicates connections between the catalogue and the passage or poem as a whole. *Georgics* 4 contains a river catalogue particularly full of links to the surrounding passage. The rivers form part of the connection between the tales of Aristaeus and Orpheus. Aristaeus must go to the source of the world's rivers in order to be directed to Proteus, who represents the power of water to effect change. There he hears about Orpheus and Eurydice, whose troubles began with a snakebite on a riverbank and ended at the ultimate river, the Styx.

The arrangement of the rivers within the catalogue also reveals a link to a conception of the world Vergil expresses elsewhere in the poem. The rivers are not listed from east to west or north to south, clockwise or counterclockwise. Instead, the list begins with northern rivers, both in Asia Minor and in Greece (Phasis, Lycus, and Enipeus), then proceeds to Italy (Tiber and Anio) and back

---

4. There exist mixed catalogues, in which some of the items are rivers and some are other aspects of the landscape. In those instances, the rivers themselves function more as simple place names than as items significant for their particular properties (e.g. Ovid, *Amores* 3.12; Propertius, *Elegies* 2.2, 3.11, 2.6.1-6).

5. On various catalogue structures, see Edwards 1980, 81-105.

6. Northrup 1980, 151-53.

7. On the *periplous* as a catalogue, see Jacob 1980, 116-19.

to Asia Minor (Hypanis and Caicus). Finally the Eridanus represents both a mythical river of the far north and the Po in northern Italy. The logic behind this list comes not from the order in which these rivers could be visited most easily, but the ethnographic principle that the ideal land lies in the middle between extremes. The Italian rivers, the Tiber and Anio, are positioned in the middle of the list, with three rivers preceding and following them. Although the Tiber and Anio are not centrally located relative to the rivers listed (geographically, they are the most western rivers mentioned in this passage), their position at the center of the catalogue makes the point that they represent an ideal of moderation, just as does Italy's claim to continuous spring in the *laudes Italiae* (*Georgics* 2.149).[8]

Propertius, like Vergil, employs a catalogue of rivers that contributes to the structure of a poem and reflects the view of the world Propertius puts forth in that poem. In *Elegies* 3.22, Propertius places lines praising Italy (19-26) between two passages on the wonders and dangers of foreign places (5-18, 27-38, respectively). Although the places mentioned do not come in geographical order, the placement of the praises of Italy at the center of the poem implies the view that part of Italy's ideal character comes from its location in the middle of the map.

In addition to the structure of the poem, the items listed as Italy's assets contribute to the picture of Italy, and in particular Rome, as the center of the world:

> hic, Anio Tiburne, fluis, Clitumnus ab Umbro
> 　　tramite, et aeternum Marcius umor opus,
> Albanus lacus et foliis Nemorensis abundans,
> 　　potaque Pollucis nympha salubris equo.

(Propertius, Elegies 3.22.23-26)

> Here, Tiburnian Anio, you flow, and Clitumnus from its Umbrian course, and the Marcian water, that eternal work, and the Alban lake and Nemi abounding in foliage, and the healthful spring, watering place of Pollux's horse.

All of the items in the catalogue consist of water and their locations suggest a convergence upon the city of Rome. The Anio and the Clitumnus are both tributaries of the Tiber and thus flow towards Rome. The Aqua Marcia is the man-made equivalent of a river, carrying water from its source in the Anio valley to the very heart of the city, the Capitoline. The three pools Propertius mentions, although not moving water, also represent motion towards the city by the order in which they are mentioned. Those outside the city, the Alban Lake and

---

8. Like the catalogue of rivers in *Georgics* 4, the catalogue of places in the *laudes Italiae* contains links to a previous passage. The order of the list in the *laudes* mentions regions in the same order in which they had been cited in *Georgics* 2.114-35, the lines immediately preceding the *laudes* (Thomas 1988, *ad Georgics* 2.136-42).

Lake Nemi, are mentioned before the *Lacus Iuturnae*.[9] The progress of the moving water mirrors the travels described in lines 5-18, but with an important difference: in Italy there is an implied destination, Rome.

Likewise, the catalogue of Gallic rivers in Ausonius's *Moselle* serves to locate the Moselle both in a geographical context and in the context of the poem. A catalogue of Gallic rivers situates the Moselle spatially, but also reinforces its place as the centerpiece of the landscape Ausonius describes. The Moselle, a difficult work to categorize, is at once panegyrical and geographical.[10] The catalogue of Gallic rivers gives us both of these aspects: as rivers in the region of the Moselle, they define its location; as rivers that accede to the Moselle's greater status, they set it in a class by itself, apart from the multitude of other waterways.

In addition, the catalogue of Gallic rivers balances the catalogue of fishes: together the two catalogues express internal and external factors that make the Moselle a marvel. Indeed, it is this exclusive focus on the river that distinguishes the *Moselle* from other works. The aspects of the river discussed resemble ethnographical writings.[11] Rivers, however, generally were part of ethnographies rather than subjects for them. Ausonius's point may be to make the microcosm of the river into a stand-alone work in much the same way Tacitus's *Germania* can be seen as a self-contained and elaborated version of an ethnography that might exist within a larger historical work. In the *laudes Italiae* (Vergil, *Georgics* 2.136-76), ethnography and geography are miniaturized. Ausonius, in the *Moselle*, expands just one aspect of ethnography and geography, the discussion of rivers, into a self-contained work. A telling reference to the *Georgics* specifies just the aspect that he expands: he refers to the Moselle gliding past city walls (*Moselle* 454-55), an evocation of *Georgics* 2.156-57. Indeed, this reference comes in a passage concerning the expansion of Ausonius's own work (*Moselle* 450-60). Even the larger work Ausonius envisions focuses on the Moselle, however.

Even when the focus widens from the Moselle itself, rivers are the topic, and none can be preferred to the river Ausonius has already made his topic. The catalogue of Gallic rivers displays a general progression from the region southeast to the region southwest of the river, effectively framing the Moselle's source and bringing the focus back to Ausonius's current topic. In this way, the poem ends on a note of departure that is actually a promise of return: Ausonius began the Moselle with an approach to the river, and he ends by anticipating another journey to this favored place.

---

9. The Alban Lake has a tunnel for outflow that eventually joins the Tiber. The 1800m tunnel was built c. 397 BC, most likely for irrigation purposes (OCD s.v. *Albanus lacus*).

10. See Green 1991, 458-60. Green emphasizes the singularity of the work, but relates aspects of it to Vergil's *Georgics* (particularly the *laudes Italiae*) and Statius's *Silvae*.

11. Ausonius's *Moselle* shares with ethnographical writings a descriptive approach to its subject. In addition, features such as its natural resources (fish, fertile soil for grapevines), a landscape conducive to a variety of human activities (boating, swimming), and its aesthetic appeal (as an ideal location for villas) are singled out for mention. Like the Hippocratic *Airs, Waters, Places*, the *Moselle* emphasizes the salubrious nature of that which it describes.

"Library" Catalogues

In addition to creating a verbal map, Vergil's catalogue of rivers in *Georgics* 4 is at once an epic device and a reference to Hellenistic scholarly traditions. Thus, although rivers and nymphs evoke the world of nature, we are better off looking for understanding in the Library at Alexandria than in the woods and streams of Italy. The catalogues of nymphs and rivers that occur in close proximity in this book recall paired catalogues of nymphs and rivers in the *Theogony* (337-70) as well as treatises on those subjects by Callimachus.[12] In addition to this content-based connection between them, the two catalogues in the *Georgics* are united by a Homeric technique, correspondences between items in two catalogues.[13] Although the nymphs Vergil lists do not have Homeric names, but rather seem to reflect Hellenistic traditions,[14] some of the organization resembles Homeric catalogue structure:

At mater sonitum thalamo sub fluminis alti
sensit. eam circum Milesia vellera Nymphae
carpebant hyali saturo fucata colore,
Drymoque Xanthoque Ligeaque Phyllodoceque,
caesariem effusae nitidam per candida colla,
[Nysaee Spioque Thaliaque Cymodoceque]
Cydippe et flava Lycorias, altera virgo,
altera tum primos Lucinae experta labores,
Clioque et Beroe soror, Oceanitides ambae,
ambae auro, pictis incinctae pellibus ambae,
atque Ephyre atque Opis et Asia Deiopea
et tandem positis velox Arethusa sagittis.
inter quas curam Clymene narrabat inanem
Volcani, Martisque dolos et dulcia furta,
aque Chao densos divum numerabat amores.
carmine quo captae dum fusis mollia pensa
devolvunt, iterum maternas impulit auris
luctus Aristaei

(Vergil, *Georgics* 4.333-50)

But his mother heard the sound from her chamber beneath the deep river. Around her, the Nymphs were plucking Milesian fleeces dyed an intense bottle-green: Drymo and Xantho and Ligea and Phyllodoce, their lustrous hair cascading down their white necks, [Nysaee and Spio and Thalia and Cymodoce] Cydippe and blonde Lycorias, the one a maiden, the other recently having experienced the first pangs of Lucina, and Clio and her sister Beroe, both daugh-

---

12. Thomas 1988, *ad Georgics* 4.333-86. Hesiod's catalogue of rivers may simply represent a selection of the rivers of the world. Gisinger (1929, 315-19) attempts to argue for a logical arrangement of the rivers, but Hesiod seems determined to juxtapose Greek and foreign rivers as well as those located far from one another.

13. The female shades that Odysseus meets in the underworld (*Odyssey* 11.225-332) correspond to the male shades he is about to encounter in 11.385-600 (Northrup 1980, 150).

14. Thomas 1988, *ad Georgics* 4.333-86.

ters of Okeanos, both outfitted in gold and dappled hides, and Ephyre and Opis and Asian Deiopea and swift Arethusa, at last having put aside her arrows. Among them Clymene was telling of Vulcan's unrequited love, and the tricks and stolen pleasures of Mars, and from Chaos onwards she was recounting the frequent loves of the gods. While the nymphs, captivated by her song, spin the soft wool with their spindles, again the lament of Aristaeus strikes his mother's ears.

Line 335, in particular, resembles the Homeric catalogue of nereids. The four names, connected by *-que*, recall the pattern of *Iliad* 18.39,[15] the line with which the Homeric catalogue begins.[16] After evoking Homer with the catalogue's opening, Vergil chooses to mention nymphs primarily known from extant works of Callimachus, rather than from Homer, a characteristic that underscores the literary and allusive nature of this catalogue.[17]

Just as Homer had linked the male and female shades in *Odyssey* 11, Vergil creates a list of rivers in which each name evokes one or more of the nymphs he catalogued only a few lines before:

omnia sub magna labentia flumina terra
spectabat diversa locis, Phasimque Lycumque,
et caput unde altus primum se erumpit Enipeus,
unde pater Tiberinus et unde Aniena fluenta
saxosusque sonans Hypanis Mysusque Caicus
et gemina auratus taurino cornua vultu
Eridanus, quo non alius per pinguia culta
in mare purpureum violentior effluit amnis.

                                             (Vergil, *Georgics* 4.366-73)

He observed all the rivers flowing under the great earth, each in its own place, the Phasis and the Lycus, and the spring from which deep Enipeus first bursts forth, and whence father Tiber comes and Anio's stream and the rocky crashing Hypanis and the Mysian Caicus and the Eridanus, gilded with twin horns on his taurine forehead, than whom no other stream flows more mightily through the rich fields into the dark sea.

Specific correspondences link the contexts of the two catalogues, emphasizing the theme of storytelling that is a feature of each passage. The identification of nymphs and rivers does not occur in a one-to-one ratio; indeed there are eight rivers and twelve nymphs, a count that frustrates attempts to make the correspondences systematic.[18] As we have seen above, the arrangement and sound of

---

15. ἔνθ᾿ ἄρ ἔην Γλαύκη τε Θάλειά τε Κυμοδόκη τε

16. In addition to recalling the beginning of the Homeric catalogue of nereids, *Georgics* 4.336 rhythmically matches *Iliad* 18.43: Δωτώ τε Πρωτώ τε Φέρουσά τε Δυναμένη τε (Thomas 1988, *ad Georgics* 4.336).

17. See Thomas's (1988) notes on specific lines for individual echoes of Callimachus.

18. Line 338, which is most likely an interpolation, may reflect a desire to simplify the numerical relationship between nymphs and rivers. The four names line 338 adds bring the number of

the first four nymph names recall Greek epic catalogues. In addition, Xantho may suggest the famous Trojan river and, thus, epic. The first three rivers Vergil mentions also evoke epic, specifically the *Iliad* and the *Argonautica*. The Phasis and Lycus are rivers of Colchis that Apollonius mentions (*Argonautica* 4.131-34), while the Enipeus, located in Thessaly, suggests Achilles. In addition, this river is described in a way similar to a characteristic Vergil mentions in his description of the nymph Phyllodoce. The poet calls attention to the head of each: Phyllodoce has hair (or foliage) poured (*effusae*, 337) over her neck, while the spring of the Enipeus, referred to as the head of the river (*caput*, 368), bursts forth (*se erumpit*, 368).

Next in the catalogue of nymphs come two pairs, Cydippe and Lycorias and then Clio and Beroe. The corresponding rivers also form a pair, the Tiber and the Anio. In the first pair of nymphs, Cydippe seems present primarily as a contrast for Lycorias. Cydippe's virginal state is a foil for an allusion to some poetic treatment of an affair Lycorias had.[19] The Tiber and Anio relate to these figures because they are a pair, but also through more specific correspondences. Lycorias is a *mater* (*Lucinae experta labores*, 340) and Vergil refers to the Tiber as *pater* (369). In addition, Lycorias receives the epithet *flava* (339), a defining trait of the Tiber.[20]

Ephyre and the Hypanis also share a characteristic: both are points of division. Ephyre is the nymph believed to have been Corinth's first inhabitant. From her name comes the appellation Ephyra, the only name by which Callimachus and Apollonius refer to Corinth, the point of division between Attica and the Peloponnese.[21] Likewise, the Hypanis, located in Scythia, was one of the boundaries cited as dividing Europe and Asia.[22]

The next two nymphs, Opis and Asian Deiopeia, correspond to the Mysian Caicus. Together, Opis and Deiopeia evoke the wealth of the East, the former with her name that sounds like *opes* and the latter with her geographical epithet. The Caicus, too, receives an epithet that locates it in Asia Minor, between Bithynia and Lydia, the latter especially known for its wealth.[23]

Rounding out each list is a figure that represents a real place (in fact both are bodies of water) as well as a myth. Arethusa's best known exploit, evading Alpheus by becoming a spring and flowing through the sea to Sicily, is not mentioned explicitly here, but may be suggested by the reference to her arrows. This attribute marks her as a woodland follower of Artemis and, thus may suggest her resolute virginity and subsequent victimization.[24] This potential for violence perhaps constitutes another characteristic shared with the Eridanus, which

---

nymphs to sixteen, double the number of rivers. As Thomas notes (1988, *ad Georgics* 4.338), the line combines nereid names from two lines of the *Iliad* (18.39-40).

19. Thomas 1988, *ad Georgics* 4.340.

20. For the Tiber as *flavus*, see Vergil, *Aeneid* 7.30; Horace *Odes* 1.2.13, 1.8.8, 2.3.18; Ovid, *Metamorphoses* 14.448, *Fasti* 6.228, *Tristia* 5.1.31.

21. Thomas 1988, *ad Georgics* 4.343.

22. Thomas 1988, *ad Georgics* 4.370.

23. Herodotus, *History* 5.49.

24. Cf. figures such as Hippolytus, Daphne, and Actaeon; Parry 1964, 268-82; Parry 1957, 3.

Vergil describes as *violentior* (373). Like Arethusa, the Eridanus recalls an
etiological myth not explicitly mentioned, in this case Phaethon. Both of these
figures are associated with two locations, as well. Arethusa has ties to Greece as
well as Sicily; Eridanus has a dual identity as the Po and as a fantastic river of
the western extreme of the world. By ending each catalogue with a name that
would evoke mythology and, perhaps, literary treatments of that mythology,
Vergil prepares readers for the connection between catalogues and narrative
frame.

The nymphs and rivers in each catalogue make up the audience for a female
character who speaks. In addition to their role as listeners, the nymphs and rivers
with their activities mirror the act of poetic composition performed by the
speaker. The nymphs spin while they listen to Clymene describe the secret love
of Mars and Venus (345-49). Woolworking frequently serves as a metaphor for
poetic composition.[25] Likewise, the flowing rivers are the backdrop for Cyrene's
account of Proteus's powers. As we have seen earlier in this chapter, flowing
water often mirrors the flow of narrative. Although Cyrene's narrative is only a
prelude to the inset tale of Orpheus and Eurydice, her mediation between Aristaeus and Proteus calls attention to the epyllion as an inset tale and also further
involves water in the telling of the story. In order to obtain the narrative from
Proteus, Aristaeus must control the seer's fluid transformations. Cyrene's location at the source of the world's rivers not only marks her as a source of information, but also emphasizes the importance of rivers, and especially of control
over rivers, whether by physical means or by imposing a structure on their
names, in telling a story.

The connections between the catalogues of nymphs and rivers call attention
to the double role of poetry in the *Georgics*. Like Clymene's tales to which the
nymphs listen, it entertains, but like Cyrene's instructions to Aristaeus, it also
imparts knowledge. By linking Clymene's story to Cyrene's instructions to her
son, Vergil highlights the functions of his didactic poetry, and of the epyllion in
particular. The correspondences between the catalogues, especially the metaphors for poetic composition contained in each, identify instructions like
Cyrene's as a poetic genre.

Chaotic Catalogues

Unlike the catalogues in the *Georgics*, which present an orderly world with Italy
or Rome at the center, some river catalogues purposely avoid any logical order.
Ovid uses geographically disordered river catalogues in two instances where the
confused sequence mirrors the events or tone of the passage. In the *Metamor-*

---

25. This metaphor may go back to the etymology of ῥαψῳδός as one who stitches together a
song (Nagy 1996, 75-76). The weaving contest between Arachne and Athena in Ovid's *Metamorphoses* (6.19-145) also relates woolworking and poetry: each tapestry tells a story that serves as an
inset narrative. Likewise, when Philomela loses the ability to speak, she makes her story known
through weaving (*Metamorphoses* 6.576-79). The Minyeides, too, spin as they tell stories (*Metamorphoses* 4.53-54).

phoses and the *Epistles from Pontus*, disordered catalogues provide variety as well as echoing aspects of the narrative.

In the *Metamorphoses*, Phaethon's fall into the Eridanus is preceded by a catalogue of the rivers of the world affected by his reckless driving of the sun's chariot (*Metamorphoses* 2.241-59). For most of the list, the names do not proceed in a logical geographical order: for instance, the catalogue jumps from northern Europe to Greece to Asia Minor with the Tanais, Peneus, and Caicus (242-43). This disorder reflects Phaethon's uncontrolled journey across the sky (232-34). Blinded by smoke and driven off course by runaway horses, Phaethon gets a capricious tour of the world's rivers. Towards the end of his journey, however, it becomes easier to follow his progress. He goes to the Nile, in the extreme south, and then to the Hebrus and Strymon in the north, before finally reaching the western rivers, the Rhine, Rhône, Po, and Tiber (254-59). These final western places foreshadow Phaethon's eventual resting place, the Eridanus (311-26).

In another instance, Ovid uses a disordered list to make clear that variety itself is a part of the reason for reciting the catalogue. In *Epistles from Pontus* 4.10.47-88, he lists fifteen rivers that dilute the Black Sea. The occasion for the catalogue is Ovid's desire to explain why the Black Sea freezes (Ovid, *Epistles from Pontus* 4.10.37-46). He asserts that the fresh water that flows into the Black Sea from the area's numerous rivers floats on top of the sea and contributes to the sea's behavior as fresh water.[26] The explanation itself is reminiscent of Lucretius, a connection suggested by Ovid's previous comparison of his endurance to items that are worn away over time (Ovid, *Epistles from Pontus* 4.10.3-8).[27] With regard to rivers that flow into the sea, however, Lucretius believed that they did not alter the composition of the sea. By asserting that the Black Sea experiences exactly that kind of change, Ovid implies that his new surroundings have a character all their own and cannot be expected to conform to familiar principles.

The foreign-sounding names in the catalogue mirror the strange situation created by their dilution of the Black Sea, supporting Ovid's point that his new home is unnatural by Roman standards. This idea parallels the poet's earlier assertion that he has experienced harsher conditions than did Odysseus (9-34). The confused order in which Ovid mentions the rivers reinforces the strangeness

---

26. Interestingly, modern study of the Black Sea supports Ovid's observations regarding its composition. This body of water has two distinct layers: an upper layer has relatively low salinity and a bottom layer has a higher salinity. The difference in composition between upper and lower layers is due, at least in part, to the influx of river water, as evidenced by the similarity in mineral composition of surface water near a river mouth to the water of the corresponding river (Degens and Ross 1974, 579-80, 102). Although today the Black Sea remains ice-free in winter, it has been known to freeze (Degens and Ross 1974, 130).

27. The passage, in fact, contains a subset of the examples Lucretius uses to demonstrate that all objects are made of particles too small to see (Lucretius, *De Rerum Natura* 1.311-24). Likewise, the explanation that river water dilutes the Black Sea recalls a Lucretian passage, but makes a different argument. In fact, Lucretius argues for the stability of the composition of the sea, despite the rivers that flow into it (Lucretius, *De Rerum Natura* 5.261-71).

of the place: even if readers knew something of the geography of the Black Sea region, this list would render the area less familiar. He lists them thus: Lycus, Sagaris, Penius, Hypanis, Cales, Halys, Parthenius, Cinases, Tyras, Thermodon, Phasis, Danapris, Melanthus, and Don (the last described but not named). We might expect the rivers to be named in a sequence representing èither a clockwise or a counterclockwise voyage around the Black Sea, but instead Ovid presents the rivers in an order seemingly without geographical considerations. Some of the names perhaps are placed near one another for verbal effect (e.g. Penius and Hypanis, Calys and Halys, Phasis and Danapris). In this way, Ovid, by drawing attention away from the places named and towards the names themselves, creates a new reality for the rivers, one in which the demands of poetry take precedence over the constraints of geography. In these lines, the world seems at once disordered and possessed of a new structure, one imposed by a poet who has so often in this work complained that he cannot conform to the rigors of his new environment.

Another purpose of the catalogue, indeed the one cited by the poet himself, is entertainment. In 67-70, Ovid explains that, in writing this poem, he has been able to forget his cares, one reason to extend the poem with a catalogue.[28] Indeed, he takes several opportunities to bring familiar myths to mind amid the abundance of foreign names. The Phasis is *Graiis . . . petite viris* (52) and Europe is referred to as *Cadmique sororem* (55). These references hint at diverting stories that could be told to pass the time, were the passage to be expanded even further.

In another instance as well, Ovid passes time with a river catalogue that also functions to emphasize the unnatural character of his immediate surroundings. In *Amores* 3.6, the poet heaps insults upon a river that denies him access to his *puella*, just one way in which Ovid claims that the river does not act in accord with its nature. As a way of appealing to the river's sympathies, he lists a number of rivers notable for their amorous exploits and suggests that this river, too, must know how it feels to be in love. Thus, the theme of the list, rivers in love, fits the subject of the poem. It serves another purpose as well, however. It acts as a didactic device by which Ovid wittily attempts to instruct the stream in proper behavior for a river.

The catalogue is framed with descriptions of the river the poet wishes to cross. In both cases, these descriptions show how this river compares unfavorably to others. In the first characterization of the river, Ovid claims that it has no bridge and that in flood it is muddy, the latter reminiscent of Callimachus's equation of the broad muddy river with undesirable poetry (*Amores* 3.6.1-8). While the river once was *parvus*, it now merits adjectives such as *turpi* and *crassas*, qualities that Callimachean poetry rejects. In addition to its similarity to undesirable poetic practices, the river lacks several important characteristics of a river (*Amores* 3.6.91-100). Without a name, source, or beneficial effects for man

---

28. Bernhardt 1986, 325.

or beast, the river's identity is called into question. Ovid implies that if it lacks essential aspects of a river, it may not merit that designation at all.

The catalogue itself, from which the uncrossable river is excluded for lack of an amorous tale to share (and for lack of a name), is the poet's torrent of words, corresponding to the river's flood. The catalogue, however, does not succeed in persuading the flood to abate, and, finally, the poet regrets expending words upon such an unworthy stream (Ovid, *Amores* 3.6.101-4).

Ovid has written a poem about a river that does not deserve one and, furthermore, he mentions it in the same breath as more famous rivers, an honor he claimed it did not deserve. By "unwittingly" granting the river a poem, Ovid implies that rivers and poetry go together no matter what. Even if Ovid enumerates characteristics that would seem to exclude the stream as a subject for poetry, the body of water inserts itself into the category simply by virtue of its flow. It is this quality that detains the poet and, thus, occasions the poem.

Catalogues of rivers, as we have seen, lend structure both to narratives and to the imagined maps their names occasion. Whether the point of the map is to give the world a particular organization or no order at all, river catalogues prompt readers to envision the world with attention called to particular locations in a specific order. Much like the words of a narrative, a catalogue of rivers guides an audience toward the author's conception of story or world. In the *Georgics*, a poem in which life itself clearly depends on the natural world, Vergil gives a vivid picture of the environment in which his poem takes place. Rivers contribute to the structure of both environment and poem.

Chapter Seven

Up the Creek: Upstream Voyages and Narrative Structure

Upstream voyages often function on two levels. On the level of plot, they are often necessary in describing travel. On the metapoetic level, they often have to do with the structure of a narrative and with issues of temporality. These ideas are particularly essential to the *Aeneid*, in which Aeneas's journey has significance that transcends his actual travel. As Aeneas arrives in Italy and must become part of a new landscape, upstream travel is an important image. In the *Aeneid*, the Tiber and its god play a role in advancing Aeneas's journey, both physically and psychologically. In addition, the river's behavior indicates that the Italian landscape favors Aeneas and his mission.

The Tiber, Time, and Memory

As Vergil suggests in *Aeneid* 3, it is not always possible or desirable to identify rivers in a new place with familiar streams. At times, rivers truly are foreign. When the Trojans must integrate themselves into their new Italian homeland, Vergil repeatedly casts their identity crisis in terms of their relationship to Italy's water, particularly the Tiber. Aeneas's first sighting of the Tiber takes the form of the quintessential first experience by an explorer with a foreign river: that of the *periplus*. In *Aeneid* 7, he catches sight of the mouth of the river as he sails up the Italian coast:

> atque hic Aeneas ingentem ex aequore lucum
> prospicit, hunc inter fluvio Tiberinus amoeno
> verticibus rapidis et multa flavus harena
> in mare prorumpit. Variae circumque supraque
> adsuetae ripis volucres et fluminis alveo
> aethera mulcebant cantu lucoque volabant.
> flectere iter sociis terraeque advertere proras
> imperat et laetus fluvio succedit opaco.

(Vergil, *Aeneid* 7.29-36)

And here from the water Aeneas saw a huge grove, <u>among which Tiberinus with his pleasing stream bursts forth, turbid with headlong rapids and much sand into the sea</u>. Above and around, varied birds accustomed to the banks were flying in the grove and they were charming the air with their singing. <u>He orders his companions to change their path and to turn the prows to land and happy he enters the shaded river</u>.

In a systematic exploration of the world by sea, rivers provide the easiest access to inland areas: on a coastal voyage, detours into rivers enable explorers to learn about regions other than the coast, thus expanding their knowledge beyond what mariners might be expected to know. Rivers provide the occasion for excursuses, in both the voyage and the narrative. In the *Periplous of the Erythraean Sea*, inland detours are taken whenever navigable rivers make them possible. The practical purpose of these side trips is often trade, but the author also takes the opportunity to describe the nature of the place, even further inland than is necessary to go for trade:

Καὶ παρ᾽ αὐτὸν ποταμός ἐστιν, <u>ἔχων εἰσαγωγὴν πλοίοις</u>, καὶ μικρὸν ἐπὶ τοῦ στόματος ἐμπόριον ῾Ωραία λεγόμενον καὶ κατὰ νώτου μεσόγειος πόλις, <u>ἔχουσα ὁδὸν ἡμερῶν ἑπτὰ ἀπὸ θαλάσσης</u>, ἐν ᾗ καὶ βασίλεια, ἡ λεγομένη <**>. Φέρει δὲ ἡ ξώρα σῖτον πολὺν καὶ οἶνον καὶ ὄρυζαν καὶ φοίνικα, πρὸς δὲ τὴν ἤπειρον οὐδὲν ἕτερον ἢ βδέλλα<ν>.

(Periplous of the Erythraean Sea 37)

And near it is a river, <u>having an entrance for ships</u>, and a short distance from its mouth is the market called Horaia and behind it is an inland city, <u>having a seven days' journey from the sea</u>, in which is the kingdom called _____. The land produces much grain and wine and rice and dates, but the mainland produces nothing other than bdella.

Such descriptions become models for Hellenistic and Roman literary treatments of expeditions, such as Apollonius's *Argonautica*, which in turn informs Vergil's description of the Tiber:

ἔνθα δ᾽ ἐπ᾽ ἠπείροιο Κυταιίδος, ἠδ᾽ ᾽Αμαραντῶν
τηλόθεν ἐξ ὀρέων πεδίοιό τε Κερκαίοιο
<u>Φᾶσις δινήεις εὐρὺν ῥόον εἰς ἅλα βάλλει.</u>
κείνου νῆ᾽ ἐλάοντες ἐπὶ προχοὰς ποταμοιο
. . .
ἐννύχιοι δ᾽ ῎Αργοιο δαημοσύνῃσιν ῞Ικοντο
Φᾶσίν τ᾽ εὐρὺ ῥέοντα, καὶ ἔσχατα πείρατα πόντου.
Αὐτίκα δ᾽ ἱστία μὲν καὶ ἐπίκριον ἔνδοθι κοίλης
ἱστοδόκης στείλαντες ἐκόσμεον· ἐν δὲ καὶ αὐτὸν
ἱστὸν ἄφαρ χαλάσαντο παρακλιδόν· <u>ὦκα δ᾽ ἐρετμοῖς
εἰσέλασαν ποταμοῖο μέγαν ῥόον· αὐτὰρ ὁ πάντῃ
καχλάζων ὑπόεικεν.</u>

(Apollonius Rhodius, Argonautica 2.399-401, 1260-66)

And here on the Cytaean mainland, and from the Amarantine mountains far off and from the Circaean plain the eddying Phasis casts a broad stream into the sea. Piloting the ship towards the mouth of that river. . . . By the ability of Argus, at night they reached the broad-flowing Phasis, and the farthest borders of the sea. And immediately they arranged the sails and sail-yard, placing them in the hollow mast-holder; and in it at once they let down the mast itself, turning it sideways; and swiftly they entered the great stream of the river with oars; but the stream splashing yielded on all sides.

By its very nature, the *periplus* tends to describe rivers and regions previously unfamiliar. Indeed, Apollonius alludes to the form when describing the Phasis, a river near the ends of the earth. By evoking the style of the periplus for his description of the Tiber, Vergil casts the Italian river as a foreign entity. Via these references, Vergil emphasizes the foreign quality Italy has for the Trojans. The alien character of this Iliadic half of the *Aeneid* mirrors the alien territory of Italy itself. The interplay of allusions unites these two ideas in the image of the Tiber.

The Trojans' arrival at the Tiber, however, differs from other examples of colonization or exploration. It is also a homecoming. Herendeen emphasizes the hints Vergil gives that the arrival at the Tiber marks Aeneas's homecoming, noting Vergilian echoes of the arrival of Odysseus at Phaeacia and Ithaca.[1] Both Aeneas and Odysseus reach their destinations at dawn. Vergil also evokes the Homeric language of dawn through his use of color. As Williams points out, *lutea* and *roseis* bring to mind two Homeric epithets for dawn, κροκόπεπλος and ῥοδοδάκτυλος.[2] In addition, Odysseus's survey of the landscape brings to mind Aeneas's sequential experience of the Italian coast.

As in *Georgics* 3, in *Aeneid* 7 Vergil pairs a river and a second proem. As Aeneas embarks upon the Italian leg of his journey, ordering a change of course that carries the Trojan ships into the Tiber, Vergil opens the second half of his poem, invoking the muse Erato. Everything about Aeneas's approach to the Tiber is auspicious: Neptune has provided favorable winds (*ventis . . . secundis*, 23) that subside just in time for Aeneas to notice the Tiber.[3] The river, described as *fluvio Tiberinus amoeno* (30), is inviting: the grove of trees, birds, and flowing water complete the *locus amoenus* suggested in line 30.[4]

Immediately following the description of this idyllic landscape comes the poet's invocation. In his appeal to the muse, Vergil takes for himself a role similar to that he has just granted Aeneas. While he invites the muse's presence, the poet himself will control the narrative, as the emphatically placed first-person *expediam* makes clear (40). After establishing this parallel between poet and hero, Vergil balances the optimistic circumstances of Aeneas's arrival at the Tiber with an unflinching summary of the struggle that awaits Aeneas a short distance upstream. This rapid change of fortune will transform the landscape as

---

1. Herendeen 1986, 55. See also Thomas 1985.
2. Williams 1987, *ad Aeneid* 7.25-36.
3. This detail is Vergil's innovation. Traditionally, Aeneas's landing was placed south of the Tiber (Williams 1987, *ad Aeneid* 7.25).
4. See Curtius 1953, 195-200 on the essential components of a *locus amoenus*.

well, a fact that Vergil may foreshadow in his proem. The phrase, *dicam horrida bella* (41), recalls the sibyl's prophecy (*bella, horrida bella, / et Thybrim multo spumantem sanguine cerno, Aeneid* 6.86-87). In that passage, the sibyl's prediction elaborates effect these wars will have on the Italian landscape: the Tiber awash in blood. By juxtaposing an idyllic image of the Tiber with a reminiscence of a particularly horrible picture of it, Vergil not only suggests the price at which Trojan occupation of the Tiber will come, but he also foreshadows the beginning of the war itself, when an idyllic river scene will turn to bloodshed as Ascanius shoots Silvia's pet stag (*Aeneid* 7.493-99).

In addition to its role as a point of embarkation both for the next stage of Aeneas's travels and for the second half of the poem, the Tiber provides a course for words and narrative. Rumor's report of the Trojans' arrival has reached the cities of Ausonia by the time Aeneas and his men complete the initial leg of their journey upstream (*Aeneid* 7.104-6). Words have flown while ships were in motion on the river and, as words and ships reach their destinations, there is a tension between idyllic setting and growing unease, similar to that achieved in the invocation.

So we see in *Aeneid* 7 rivers supporting travel not only of Vergil's characters, but also of information. In a number of instances they mark important moments in the arrival of war in Italy. The parallels between Aeneas's embarkation on a river journey and Vergil's own embarkation on the second half of his epic suggest that we see the river as a conveyer of the narrative itself. This link becomes even stronger in *Aeneid* 8.

In *Aeneid* 8, travel on the Tiber begins again, and again has a narratological function. We first see Aeneas troubled, his mind rushing here and there as if carried on turbulent water: first Vergil uses a metaphor (*magno curarum fluctuat aestu*, 19) and then a simile comparing Aeneas's mind to light that dances as it is reflected on water (22-25). Despite the restlessness of his mind, Aeneas finally lies still, asleep on the riverbank, until Tiberinus appears to him in a dream and spurs him to action. The god offers Aeneas two things, a prophecy and aid in traveling upstream: both Tiberinus's words and his water facilitate Aeneas's mission.[5]

The river god's help consists of stopping the Tiber's current so that the Trojans can sail upstream without difficulty. The Trojans' progress contrasts with the river's stalled flow. Indeed, the narrative of the growing conflict between Aeneas and Turnus remains in suspended animation while we experience a literary and geographical excursus concerning another local king, Evander. Indeed, much of *Aeneid* 8 can stand alone, as it constitutes a pause between the opening of hostilities and preparations for battle in *Aeneid* 7 and the battle sequences of subsequent books. Just as an excursus is at once a pause in the action and a move outside the primary narrative, Aeneas's trip combines a stationary river with the characters' travel.

---

5. This is a good example of a river having both temporal and spatial significance, attributes that will be relevant in considering the Palestrina Nile Mosaic.

The lines that describe the journey's beginning express the necessity of still water for advancing Aeneas's knowledge:

Thybris ea fluvium, quam longa est, nocte tumentem
leniit, et tacita refluens ita substitit unda,
mitis ut in morem stagni placidaeque paludis
sterneret aequor aquis, remo ut luctamen abesset.
ergo iter inceptum celerant rumore secundo:
labitur uncta vadis abies; mirantur et undae,
mitatur nemus insuetum fulgentia longe
scuta virum fluvio pictasque innare carinas.

(Vergil, *Aeneid* 8.86-93)

All night long, the Tiber calmed his swollen current, and flowing back, stopped thus with silent wave, such that as soft as a pool or still marsh he calmed the water's surface, so that oars might not struggle. Therefore with encouraging shouts they speed the journey now begun: the ships sealed with pitch glide on the waters; the waves marvel, and the unaccustomed grove marvels at the men's shields flashing far off and the painted ships traveling on the river.

The unnatural stillness of the Tiber's current enables the Trojans to hasten their journey, which is necessary for the story to move forward. Words, in this case spoken by amazed onlookers, also seem to help. In this passage, *secundo* clearly means "favorable" or "encouraging," but in the context of the river, its navigational connotation may also be present, suggesting a following wind. An echo of 8.56-57 also suggests this interpretation. In those lines, Tiberinus promises the help that he delivers in 86-90 (*ipse ego te ripis et recto flumine ducam, / adversum remis superes subvectus ut amnem*, 56-57). Here, he intimates that the Trojans, with his help, will overcome an adverse current. When Tiberinus stays the current, there is no struggle with the oars, and the encouragement of onlookers spurs them on as well. *Secundo* contrasts with *adversum*, implicitly likening the shouts of the crowd to a favorable wind.

As verbal encouragement from spectators provides impetus for the journey, the river becomes an observer (*miratur et undae*, 91). This reversal of roles calls attention to the issue of progress. While the river remains still, the story progresses, although this new episode interrupts the narrative of the conflict with the Latins. In order for Aeneas to achieve his fated future, he must understand more about the origins of the people with whom he is coming into contact, as well as receive additional prophecies.

Travel upstream often represents travel back in time.[6] In addition to the analogy between the current of a river and the passage of time, in which travel against the current represents motion back in time, the link between a trip upstream and previous times has a basis in ethnography. Inland peoples were viewed as more primitive culturally than those living at the coast. Coastal peoples had more exposure to foreigners and, thus, could acquire goods and knowl-

---

6. See below on the Palestrina Nile Mosaic.

edge of other cultures.[7] Perhaps this real tendency to perceive inland peoples as isolated from Greek and Roman culture, and thus primitive, contributes to the perception that travel upstream is like travel back in time. Here, we are reminded of this ethnographical concept by the surprised reaction of the landscape to the ships traveling on the Tiber. This astonishment suggests that this region is not accustomed to warfare (*nemus insuetum*) and, thus, that the area exists at an earlier stage of civilization.[8]

We see similar themes in the *Odyssey* and the *Argonautica*, both of which Vergil alludes to in this passage. In *Odyssey* 5, Odysseus is saved from death at sea after his prayers to a river god are answered when the river quiets its waters and receives him into its stream:

> ὣς φάθ', ὁ δ' αὐτίκα παῦσεν ἑὸν ῥόον, ἔσχε δὲ κῦμα,
> πρόσθε δέ οἱ ποίησε γαλήνην, τὸν δ' ἐσάωσεν
> ἐς ποταμοῦ προχοάς.
>
> (Homer, *Odyssey* 5.451-53)

So he spoke, and the river stopped his current, and stayed his wave, and made calm water before him, and gave him refuge at the mouth of the river.

Note that ἔσχε δὲ κῦμα and *substitit unda* (*Aeneid* 8.87) have the same meter and meaning. Homer's unnamed river god performs a function similar to Tiberinus: he calms his waters in order to make an upstream journey possible. Odysseus's upstream voyage, like Aeneas's, affords the hero a means of navigating an unknown land by imposing a path on seemingly trackless wilderness. It also leads him to an encounter with people who have an idyllic lifestyle. Both Odysseus and Aeneas receive help toward completing their missions from the people with whom these rivers put them in contact.

Vergil's Arcadians, like the Phaeacians, live at a remove from the rest of the world. The Arcadians are associated with the pastoral world, a sphere removed from ships and warfare. The Arcadians, although they are not unfamiliar with war (they provide Aeneas with troops), react with fear to the Trojans' approach:

> ut celsas videre rates atque inter opacum
> adlabi nemus et tacitos incumbere remis,
> terrentur visu subito cunctique relictis
> consurgunt mensis.
>
> (Vergil, *Aeneid* 8.107-10)

When they saw the tall ships glide through the dark grove and men bend to silent oars, they feel sudden fear at the sight and all rise and abandon the tables.

---

7. Caesar describes the Belgae as a hardy people, owing to their inaccessibility to merchants who might supply them with luxury items. They also lack the refinement of those who are more accessible, however (*absunt longissime a cultu atque humanitate Provinciae*, Caesar, *Gallic War* 1.1.3).

8. In the succession of ages, war is a feature of the Iron Age, absent from earlier times, particularly the Golden Age.

There is no indication that they fear the Trojans because they have never seen ships before, but their response suggests that a warlike interruption of their worship of Hercules is a unique event. Their astonishment mirrors that of the landscape (*Aeneid* 8.81-93).

The *Argonautica* contains another model for Aeneas's journey up the Tiber. Apollonius Rhodius, too, connects river travel with remote locations and times. In *Argonautica* 4, Jason and his men must return to Greece via a different route than the one they traveled to Colchis. Rather than going via Okeanos, as they had on their outward journey, the Argonauts use the Ister, which goes through Northern Europe as opposed to skirting it. The principle behind this alternate route involves connections between the major rivers of the world (Apollonius Rhodius, *Argonautica* 4.282-93). The Ister, described as an inlet of Okeanos, immediately suggests the possibility that all rivers are connected.

Apollonius describes the shepherds who live along the Ister as terrifed by the Argo, since they have never seen a seafaring ship before:

> εἰαμενῇσι δ' ἐν ἄσπετα πώεα λεῖπον
> ποιμένες ἄγραυλοι νηῶν φόβῳ, οἷά τε θῆρας
> ὀσσόμενοι πόντου μεγακήτεος ἐξανιόντας·
> οὐ γάρ πω ἁλίας γε πάρος ποθὶ νῆας ἴδοντο
> (Apollonius Rhodius, *Argonautica* 4.316-19)

And the rustic shepherds left their countless flocks in the fields for fear of the ships, as if they had seen beasts emerging from the monster-breeding sea; for they had never seen ocean-going vessels before.

The Argo was often described as being the first ship, but by this point in the poem, much of the world has seen the Argo. These shepherds, however, are isolated enough from the Mediterranean that this is their first view. Until they see the ship, they remain part of a world before the advent of commerce and warfare, a world different from the one now occupied by the Argonauts. In the Argonauts' outward voyage, they did not encounter any local inhabitants along the Thermodon. The reporting of the reaction of the natives along their return course makes that leg of the journey seem that much more remote. The shift in perspective from that of Jason and his crew to that of the shepherds continues with a list of other native peoples all along the river that likens Jason and the Argonauts to colonizers who change the landscape they encounter.[9] Similarly, the Italian landscape and the Arcadians represent a shift in perspective from Aeneas and the Trojans, which likewise brings to mind the impending incursion of war. In addition, the Ister functions as a symbolic connection between Jason and Medea, since one of its mouths faces Colchis and the other faces Greece.[10]

In addition to the suggestions of primitivism provided by the response of landscape and inhabitants to Aeneas's arrival, the trip up the Tiber involves ear-

---

9. Williams 1991, 126-27.
10. Williams 1991, 125.

lier times in the historical, as well as the cultural, sense. Aeneas's trip upstream to visit Evander results in a description of the site of Rome in the Golden Age. Aeneas is eager to learn the history of the land he now calls home (*Aeneid* 8.310-12). The site of Rome, however, occasions information about the future as well as about the past. In addition to *virum monimenta priorum* (8.312), Evander shows Aeneas locations that will become significant to future Romans (8.337-50). For Aeneas, this is a glimpse of the future, but for Vergil's audience it continues the trip through Rome's past. The journey combines memory and prophecy and perhaps questions the distinction: what is remembered and what is predicted depends on where in the stream of time the observer sits. Aeneas's future is the reader's past, accessed by experiencing Vergil's poem. Aeneas is able to access the past as well as the future by sailing on a stilled river, a symbol that represents not only the ease with which he accesses the past but also his ability to stand temporarily outside the passage of time.

Spatial and temporal again come together in Lucan. Julius Caesar pledges to give up civil war if he gains knowledge of the source of the Nile (*Civil War* 10.188-92). The origin of the river is a metaphor for the origins of civilization and of the world. It seems that an understanding of these things would bring with it the power Caesar seeks. Or perhaps control of the Nile, through mastery of its source, would give Caesar command of Egypt, or intellectual supremacy would quell his desire for political power.[11]

Travel upstream can reveal cultures that represent an earlier stage in the development of those located closer to the coast, as well as the river's own history, in the form of its source. This search for origins is a metaphor for the inquiry into the roots of civilization in general or of a particular people such as the Romans. In the *Argonautica* and the *Aeneid*, a journey upstream enables the characters to glimpse a time that cannot be recaptured: the Golden Age. The river, however, connects this remote time with the poems' present.

Rivers and words are both involved in the manipulation of time and space. An author controls the beginning, end, and forward motion of his narrative. He can also undercut those seeming absolutes, creating a false ending or a narrative that loops back upon itself. Rivers, with their changeable nature, are an image well suited to expressing the flexibility fiction can bring to time and space. Indeed, the river as a metaphor for the passage of time appears several times in Roman poetry. Horace envisions the course of a person's life as a river (*Odes* 3.29.33-41). Ovid, too, likens time to flowing water. In the *Ars Amatoria*, he comments that time, like river water, flows in only one direction and, once it has passed, cannot be recalled (3.62). In the *Metamorphoses*, time is like a river because of its inexorable progress and eternal renewal. Just as time passes constantly, a river cannot stop its course as each wave is pushed onwards by the wave that follows it (15.176-85).

---

11. Lucan also describes Alexander the Great as being jealous of the Nile (*Civil War* 10.272-73).

Roman art also provides examples of the association of rivers with time. As we shall see, the Palestrina Nile Mosaic and Trajan's Column invite viewers to travel back in time as they experience the visual narratives these works present.

Time Travel on the Nile

The Palestrina Nile Mosaic combines narrative and catalogue just as we have seen literary works do. Although the two may seem to occupy separate registers of the mosaic, the Nile forges links between them. The upper portion of the mosaic is occupied by a rocky landscape filled with numerous animals, labeled with Greek names. The lower register contains a number of vignettes amid the Nile flood.

The mosaic, probably made in the first century BC, was found in the Sanctuary of Fortuna in ancient Praeneste. Between 1624 and 1626, it was removed in sections, which resulted in some uncertainty as to the correct arrangement of the pieces.[12] The basic division between wilderness and civilization, however, seems secure.

Ferrari offers an interpretation that combines geography and history as significant ideas behind the conception of the mosaic. The mosaic's location in an apse that may have formed part of a library insures that the viewer experiences the piece from bottom to top (according to its current display). In looking at the mosaic in this way, the viewer begins his journey through the mosaic at the harbor in Alexandria and travels upstream to the river's mysterious sources.[13] The journey is marked by changes in the topography from floodplain to mountain and of the inhabitants from light skinned to dark skinned. Ferrari adds that the trip represents time travel as well. The viewer goes back through history to a time before civilization.[14] Time and space are shown as continuous, as the river's bends lead the eye through the composition.[15] Water also makes the transition between lower and upper register, although the contrast is clear. In the lower portion of the mosaic, land appears as islands in the flood, while in the upper part, water forms pools surrounded by land.

In the upper portion, while water is present, the focus shifts to the animals, which are highlighted by labels. The presence of text calls attention to the remoteness of these creatures from everyday experience: the viewer requires names to identify what is depicted. As Ferrari observes, it also alludes to the

---

12. See Meyboom 1995, 3-41 for images, background information, and a description of the fragments.

13. Ferrari 1999, 363.

14. Ferrari 1999, 366. Mitchell (1994, 17) connects historical narrative in depictions of landscapes with "the discourse of imperialism." Just as history moves forward in time, empires move outward in space. In the Nile Mosaic, Greco-Roman influence on Egyptian culture is evident toward the bottom of the mosaic, which signifies not only the part of Egypt closest to the Mediterranean, but also the recent history of that land.

15. Ramage and Ramage 1991, 67.

process of discovery, during which naming must occur.[16] The variety of animals the mosaic visually catalogues alludes to the generative power of the Nile.[17]

In the lower portions of the mosaic, variety persists, but in a narrative format. Water is the backdrop and connects scenes that are related thematically as well as topographically. We see activities associated with the Nile flood that follow the course of the river.[18] As Ferrari points out, the depiction has features in common with a *ges periodos* or *chorographia*.[19]

These genres, the ges periodos and the chorographia, have much in common with catalogues. They may present information in lists, without a narrative structure. Just so, in the upper portion of the Nile Mosaic, the presentation resembles a catalogue. The animals with their labels are at once connected by the river and depicted as discrete entities. In the lower portion, vignettes dominate, and it is easier to imagine a narrative describing events or a journey. This more elaborate structure mirrors the higher level of civilization present in the lower portion of the mosaic. The object that marks the boundary between the upper and lower sections is the Nilometer. This device makes it possible to exploit the Nile flood for irrigation, allowing for civilized life on the Delta.[20] Indeed, this is exactly what the mosaic depicts, civilized life during the flood.

There is, however, continuity between the two parts. Animals are present in the lower part and water appears in the upper register. Indeed, continuity is one of the primary functions of the water. Just as when it is used in a literary setting to represent narrative, water here connects the vignettes and leads the viewer from one to the next.[21] Water also unites the composition in another way. Originally, the mosaic was displayed under a thin layer of water that emanated from a hidden source in the artificial cave for which the mosaic provided a floor.[22]

These similarities between the role of the Nile in the mosaic and literary uses of rivers are not surprising, given the likelihood that the mosaic was displayed in a library. Ferrari argues that the Lower Complex at Palestrina should be seen as a library and the two mosaics that occupy symmetrical apses as representations of a *chorographia* and a *periplous*.[23] The Nile Mosaic, and the Nile itself, are a perfect way of visually representing intellectual inquiry. The river guides the viewer through a strange land that contains foreign customs, scientific

---

16. Ferrari 1999, 365.

17. Herodotus deals with the variety of unfamiliar animals in Libya by cataloguing (*History* 4.191-92). As Romm notes, this catalogue creates a "brief, imagistic portrait" of the area, which he treats in less detail than Egypt (1992, 92). In addition, the catalogue form, by its matter-of-fact nature, can counteract the disbelief such fantastic animals might engender (Romm 1992, 93).

18. According to Ferrari's reconstruction. Meyboom arranges the scenes differently, to reflect ritual rather than topography (1995, 3-7).

19. Ferrari 1999, 376-77.

20. See Strabo, *Geography* 17.48 on the function of the Nilometer. The devices could be shaped as wells, corridors with stairs, or rectangular basins. The well shape implies that this is either the one located at Assuan or a generic Nilometer, because Roman depictions are always in the shape of wells (Meyboom 1995, 52).

21. The same device occurs on an oriental rug displayed in the Bryn Mawr College library.

22. Ferrari 1999, 367-68.

23. See Ferrari 1999, 381 on the identification of the fish mosaic as a *periplous*.

advances like the Nilometer, and strange animals. The hidden water source in the artificial cave, to be identified with the cave of the Muses,[24] suggests a source of knowledge, precisely the function of the library as a whole. Indeed, the source of the Nile instantly prompts literary references: Herodotus discussed the problem, and it persisted as a geographical puzzle.[25]

Trajan's Column can be read as an upstream journey as well. The narrative follows a spiral path and proceeds from the bottom to the top of the column. The personification of the Danube appears at the beginning and functions as a starting point both spatially and conceptually.[26] In one of the first scenes in the sequence, the Danube rises from his stream to regard the Roman soldiers making their preparations.[27] The support of this foreign landscape for the Roman endeavor is implied by the physical support the river god offers as he holds up the bridge of boats with his hand.[28]

From this auspicious beginning, the narrative continues upwards on the column and inland as the Romans extend their territory. In this way, narrative follows geography and geography shapes the viewers' experience of that narrative. The scenes necessarily become smaller as they near the top of the column, much like a river is narrower near its source. Coins of Trajan show the column topped with a statue of the emperor, a fitting *caput*, as he was the ultimate source of the expedition. Trajan's Column differs from the Nile Mosaic in that the narrative proceeds forward in time as it ascends the column and moves inland. Memory still plays an important role, however. The sequential scenes suggest an annalistic style, the goal of which is to record for posterity.

The river lends itself naturally to representing poetic inspiration and composition. As is evidenced by its use as a metaphor for the passage of time, Roman writers recognized continuity and directional motion as essential qualities of the river. As we have seen, both of these characteristics apply to narrative as well. Aeneas's journey up the Tiber in *Aeneid* 8 provides a particularly clear example of the way in which river and poetry interact. The idea of a river as a mediator in our experience of a narrative is not limited to literature, but occurs in art as well, as evidenced by the Palestrina Nile Mosaic and Trajan's Column.

---

24. Ferrari 1999, 374.

25. Herodotus seems to have devoted considerable intellectual effort to researching the sources of the Nile (*History* 2.28-33). He claims to have heard one answer to the question of its sources, though he doubts its reliability. In addition, he says that he travelled as far as Elephantine himself, and he describes several other expeditions. This research, however, was unable to satisfy his curiosity: at 4.53, he asserts that the Nile and the Scythian Borysthenes are the only two rivers whose sources no Greek knows. Lucan expresses the view that not only is the source of the Nile unknown, it is unknowable (*Civil War* 10.130-93, 263-67). Ptolemy identifies the location of the Nile's source with confidence (*Geography* 4.8) and his identification matches modern observation (DeFilippi 1908, 292). See also Schama 1995, 262.

26. For images see Settis 1988.

27. Scene iii Cichorius; Settis 1988, 264.

28. This attitude of acceptance on the part of the river signals the support the Roman expedition has from the land, an interpretation supported by depictions of the Danube on Trajan's coins, which show the river god kneeling on a female Dacian (Braund 1996, 46).

Perhaps in visual narratives, viewers rely even more on guidance of that type, as words are not present to provide an automatic framework.

In the literary and artistic environment, the river represents a connection between present and past, just as in the cultural framework rivers connect human beings to the universe, to the gods, and to one another. The river is a way of getting from the past to the present (or vice versa) and from the beginning to the end of a narrative. Once initiated, a story must have the continuity that a river represents. Otherwise its identity as poetic or artistic creation will be lost. As we have seen, rivers like the Tiber in the *Aeneid* underline the role of the poet in moderating the creative process.

Chapter Eight

Overflow: The Reception of River Motifs

The significance accorded rivers in classical literature and art persists in later portrayals, both in terms of their cultural role and their function as a literary device. Thorough treatments of rivers in post-classical literature and art appear in books by Herendeen and Schama. Herendeen focuses on the Renaissance, while Schama undertakes a more general cultural study. I add a few parallels particularly relevant to the classical depictions of rivers treated in the preceding pages.

These later works were, of course, created in the context of the Christian associations of water. The meaning of water and rivers in Christian tradition is not independent of classical ideas about rivers, however, as the Christian tradition has its roots in the classical world. The purifying force of water is clear from its role in baptism. We can see in this ritual the idea that contact with water produces a change as well.

In Joseph Conrad's *Heart of Darkness*, a river is not only the path on which the mysterious African landscape is explored and, thus, the path the narrative follows, but also provides a link between reality and written word. The appearance of the river in a book motivates the main character to travel to the Belgian Congo:

> Now when I was a little chap I had a passion for maps. I would look for hours at South America, or Africa, or Australia, and lose myself in all the glories of exploration. At that time there were many blank spaces on the earth, and when I saw one that looked particularly inviting on a map (but they all look that) I would put my finger on it and say, When I grow up I will go there . . .
>
> True, by this time it was not a blank space any more. It had got filled since my boyhood with rivers and lakes and names. It had ceased to be a blank space of delightful mystery—a white patch for a boy to dream gloriously over. It had become a place of darkness. But there was in it one river especially, a mighty big river, that you could see on the map, resembling an immense snake uncoiled, with its head in the sea, its body at rest curving afar over a vast country, and its tail lost in the depths of the land. And as I looked at the map of it in a shop-window it fascinated me as a snake would a bird—a silly little bird.
>
> (Conrad, *Heart of Darkness*, ch. 1)

This river exemplifies the foreignness of the landscape: a European man is no more a match for the African river than a "silly little bird" is for an "immense snake." The character who falls prey to Africa, Kurtz, demonstrates how much the place can change the man. When the novella ends with a glimpse at Kurtz before he went to Africa, we realize that the foreign place had transformed him completely. In *Heart of Darkness* the river acts as a metaphor for the entire landscape, in response to which Kurtz experiences a radical change in character. This idea resembles the ethnographical concept that people are best suited to their local water and may be adversely affected by foreign water.

Nevertheless, explorers and colonists discover new places and strange landscapes. As Schama notes, rivers are the inroads of imperialism.[1] Although the negative connotations of such actions are certainly evident, not all experiences are so reminiscent of *Heart of Darkness*. Literary and artistic representations of the encounter with strange rivers also reveal strategies for understanding and adapting to new places. The portrayal of rivers' responses to newcomers is one way in which literary authors dramatize the integration of people into a foreign place.[2]

In *Heart of Darkness*, the differences between the African river as a line on a map and as a real body of water are striking. On the map the space is white; the actual place is described as dark. The map's whiteness matches the innocence of the main character. Upon experiencing the landscape, innocence comes into contact with evil.

The idea that a circular river can exist also proves to be a persistent notion. A particularly extravagant use of the round river occurs in Joyce's *Finnegans Wake*. Full of classical references and even Greek and Latin words, this work begins with moving water. The first word, the emphatically lower-case "riverrun," sets the reader on a journey:

> riverrun, past Eve and Adam's, from swerve of shore to bend of bay, brings us by a commodius vicus of recirculation back to Howth Castle and Environs.
>
> (Joyce, *Finnegans Wake*)

The beginning of the journey, however, may not coincide with the book's opening: instead the process is one of "recirculation back to Howth Castle and Environs." For the origin of this return trip, we must look to the end of the work, where the last sentence trails off before its end and picks up with the work's fragmentary opening sentence:

> End here. Us then. Finn again! Take. Bussoftlhee, mememormee! Till thousandsthee. Lps. The keys to. Given! A way a lone a last a loved a long the
>
> (Joyce, *Finnegans Wake*)

---

1. Schama 1995, 5.
2. See above on colonization.

The book's final word, "the," makes it impossible to see the conclusion as final. The ending contains other clues as well: the statement, "End here," is immediately undercut by the continuation of the prose. In addition, the pun, "Finn again," points to iteration as a key to the work.[3]

To complete both final and initial sentences, we must join them, making the book an unbroken circle of prose that demands rereading. This cyclical structure reflects the Viconian view of history, to which Joyce subscribed.[4] Vico envisioned history as consisting of three cultural ages (of gods, heroes, and men) followed by a fourth, brief age of divine providence that sets the cycle in motion again.[5] For Vico, too, the river was an important image, representing everything in nature because everything constantly changes.[6] For Joyce, a cyclical history of the world finds expression in a round river. The circular shape of this narrative also suggests its completeness. Like the river Okeanos in Greek cosmology, the structure of *Finnegans Wake* indicates that the work encompasses the whole world. Indeed, the number of words, languages, names, places, and themes contained within it make it seem like an exhaustive repository of the author's (if not mankind's) knowledge.[7]

The round river can represent limits just as surely as it can indicate completeness. In the tale of Paul Bunyan and the Round River, loggers float logs endlessly downstream until they realize they have passed Bunyan's camp several times and conclude that the river is round. This story is an exaggeration of the embarrassing discovery by loggers that they have guided their logs into an inlet and must turn around and float them out again the way they came.[8] Nevertheless, the tale becomes one of a journey that has its ending as its beginning. The repetitions employed in one telling reflect that iteration:

> We cut our logs and stacked 'em on the river. And in the spring when the ice and snow was off, we started a spring drive a logs. Well we drove those logs down stream for a couple of weeks. And we come to a set of camps that looked just like Old Paul's camps. So, we drove for a couple of weeks more, and we come to another set that looked just like Old Paul's, so we started for a third week, and we begin to think there might be somethin' wrong. So when two weeks is up and we come to the set of camps again, we went ashore, and sure enough, it was Old Paul's camp! And there we'd been draggin' those logs around and round, around and round, around and round the river all that time and never knowed no difference. Didn't know that that river didn't have no beginnin' and no end.
>
> (Perry Allen, "The Round River Drive")[9]

---

3. See Burrell 1996, 15.

4. Joyce claimed that Vico's *New Science* was the key to understanding *Finnegans Wake* (Verene 1987, ix).

5. Tindall 1969, 30.

6. Fáj 1987, 24.

7. Frye 1987, 6.

8. Hoffman 1983, 173 n. 40.

9. Hoffman 1983, 37-38.

Listeners to the tale must hear information repeated just as the loggers had to see the same scenery over and over. The Round River has become for these characters the whole world, one from which there seems to be no exit, despite their knowledge that other places must lie beyond.

Finnegans Wake and "The Round River Drive" both marry circular rivers with circular narrative devices. Whether the work as a whole is cyclical, prompting a repeated experience of the text or the story contains internal repetitions, both seem to frustrate attempts to reach the narrative's end. To take Okeanos as a model, circularity prevents an ending and also reveals the logical difficulties occasioned by an end: if the known world has a terminus, then we can ask what lies beyond it. In a circular structure, the end always returns the traveler to the beginning of the journey.

In a literary environment, rivers contribute not only to the setting, but also provide important opportunities for self-referential comment by the author. Vergil demonstrates this technique particularly clearly. In the *Eclogues*, *Georgics*, and *Aeneid*, rivers underline structuring principles of the works. In addition, rivers mediate between poetry and poet, encompassing not only the poet's inspiration, but also the substance of the poetry itself, as distinct from the figure of the poet.

This symbolic reading of rivers does not exist in a vacuum. Essential ancient beliefs about the nature of rivers inform the symbolic value they acquire. Originative and containing the potential for infinite variety, markers of transition, and badges of identity, rivers impose paths and patterns on time and space. In much the same way, an author creates a linear narrative from disparate story elements and shapes his audience's experience of the world he fashions.

Bibliography

Anderson, W. S., ed. *Ovid's Metamorphoses Books 6-10*. Norman: University of Oklahoma Press, 1972.

Austin, C. "Notes on the Pride of Halicarnassus." *Zeitschrift für Papyrologie und Epigraphie* 126 (1999) 92.

Bartók, B. and A. B. Lord. *Serbo-Croatian Folk Songs: Texts and Transcriptions of Seventy-Five Folk Songs from the Milman Parry Collection, and a Morphology of Serbo-Croatian Folk Melodies*. New York: Columbia University Press, 1951.

Baswell, C. *Virgil in Medieval England: Figuring the Aeneid from the Twelfth Century to Chaucer*. New York: Cambridge University Press, 1995.

Bernhardt, U. *Die Funktion der Kataloge in Ovids Exilpoesie*. New York: Olms Weidmann, 1986.

Bömer, F., ed. *Die Fasten: P. Ovidius Naso*. Heidelberg: C. Winter, 1957-1958.

Borca, F. *Terra Mari Cincta: Insularità e Cultura Romana*. Rome: Carocci, 2000.

Braund, D. "River Frontiers in the Environmental Psychology of the Roman World." In *The Roman Army in the East*, edited by D. L. Kennedy. *Journal of Roman Archaeology*, Supplementary Series no. 18 (1996): 43-47.

Brinton, A. C. *Mapheus Vegius and his Thirteenth Book of the Aeneid*. Stanford, Calif.: Stanford University Press, 1930.

Buchheit, V. *Vergil über die Sendung Roms: Untersuchungen zum Bellum Poenicum und zur Aeneis*. Heidelberg: C. Winter, 1963.

Burkert, W. *Greek Religion: Archaic and Classical*, tr. J. Raffan. Oxford: Blackwell, 1985.

Burnet, J. *Early Greek Philosophy*. New York: Meridian Books, 1957.

Burrell, H. *Narrative Design in Finnegans Wake: The Wake Lock Picked*. Gainesville: University Press of Florida, 1996.

Cameron, A. *Callimachus and His Critics*. Princeton, N.J.: Princeton University Press, 1995.

Clare, R. J. *The Path of the Argo: Language, Imagery, and Narrative in the Argonautica of Apollonius Rhodius*. New York: Cambridge University Press, 2002.

Clausen, W., ed. *Virgil: Eclogues*. New York: Oxford University Press, 1995.

Cole, S. G. "The Uses of Water in Greek Sanctuaries." In *Early Greek Cult Practice,* edited by R. Hägg, N. Marinatos, and G. C. Nordquist. Stockholm: Paul Aströms Förlag, 1988.

Colebrook, C. *New Literary Histories: New Historicism and Contemporary Criticism*. New York: St. Martin's Press, 1997.

Coleman, R., ed. *Virgil: Eclogues*. New York: Cambridge University Press, 1989.

Curtius, E. R. *European Literature and the Latin Middle Ages*, tr. W. R. Trask. New York: Pantheon Books, 1953.

Dalley, S. *Myths from Mesopotamia: Creation, the Flood, Gilgamesh, and Others*. New York: Oxford University Press, 1991.

DeFilippi, F. *Ruwenzori: An Account of the Expedition of H.R.H. Prince Luigi Amedeo of Savoy Duke of the Abruzzi*. New York: E. P. Dutton and Company, 1908.

Degens, T. and D. A. Ross, ed. *The Black Sea: Geology, Chemistry, and Biology*. Tulsa, Okla.: American Association of Petroleum Geologists, 1974.

de Romilly, J. *Magic and Rhetoric in Ancient Greece*. Cambridge, Mass.: Harvard University Press, 1975.

Detienne, M. and J. P. Vernant. *Cunning Intelligence in Greek Culture and Society*, tr. J. Lloyd. Chicago: University of Chicago Press, 1991.

Diels, H. *Herakleitos von Ephesos: Griechische und Deutsch*. Berlin: Weidmannsche Buchhandlung, 1901.

Dodds, E. R., ed. *Euripides Bacchae*. Oxford: Clarendon Press, 1977.

Dougherty, C. *The Poetics of Colonization: from City to Text in Archaic Greece.* New York: Oxford University Press, 1993.

Dunbabin, T. J. "Galaesus." *Classical Quarterly* 41 (1947): 93-94.

Dyson, J. T. "*Sic Denique Victor*: An Interpretation of the End of Virgil's *Aeneid*." Diss. Harvard University, 1993.

———. *King of the Wood*. Norman: University of Oklahoma Press, 2001.

Edwards, M. W. "The Structure of Homeric Catalogues." *Transactions of the American Philological Association* 110 (1980): 81-105.

Fáj, A. "Vico's Basic Law of History in *Finnegans Wake*." In *Vico and Joyce*, edited by D. P. Verene. Albany: State University of New York Press, 1987.

Fantham, E. "*Sunt Quibus in Plures Ius Est Transire Figuras*: Ovid's Self-Transformers in the *Metamorphoses*." *Classical World* 87 (1993): 21-36.

Farnell, L. R. *The Cults of the Greek States*. Oxford: Clarendon Press, 1896-1909.

Ferguson, J. *Greek and Roman Religion: A Source Book*. Park Ridge, N.J.: Noyes Press, 1980.

Ferrari, G. "The Geography of Time: The Nile Mosaic and the Library at Praeneste." *Ostraka* 8, no. 2 (1999): 359-86.

Ferrero, L. *Storia del Pitagorismo nel Mondo Romano*. Turin: Università di Torino, Facolta di Lettere e Filosofia, Fondazione Parini-Chirio, 1955.

Forbes Irving, P. M. C. *Metamorphosis in Greek Myths*. New York: Oxford University Press, 1990.

Fränkel, H. *Ovid: A Poet Between Two Worlds*. Berkeley: University of California Press, 1945.

Frankfort, H., H. A. Frankfort, J. A. Wilson, T. Jacobsen, and W. A. Irwin. *The Intellectual Adventure of Ancient Man: An Essay on Speculative Thought in the Ancient Near East*. Chicago: University of Chicago Press, 1967.

Frye, N. "Cycle and Apocalypse in *Finnegans Wake*." In *Vico and Joyce*, edited by D. P. Verene. Albany: State University of New York Press, 1987.

Galinsky, K. "The Speech of Pythagoras at Ovid's *Metamorphoses* 15.75-478." *Papers of the Liverpool Latin Seminar* 10 (1998): 313-36.

Garbarino, G. *Roma e la Filosofia Greca dalle Origini alla Fine del II Secolo A.C.* Turin: G. B. Paravia, 1973.

Giannini, A., ed. *Paradoxographorum Graecorum Reliquiae*. Milan: Istituto Editoriale Italiano, 1966.

Gisinger, F. "Zur Geographie bei Hesiod." *Rheinisches Museum für Philologie* 78 (1929): 315-19.

Goodfellow, M. S. "North Italian Rivers and Lakes in the *Georgics*." *Vergilius* 27 (1981): 12-22.

Goold, G. P., ed. *Propertius: Elegies*. Cambridge, Mass.: Harvard University Press, 1990.

Gransden, K. W., ed. *Aeneid: Book VIII*. New York: Cambridge University Press, 1976.

Green, P., tr. with introduction, commentary and glossary. *The Argonautika by Apollonius Rhodius*. Berkeley: University of California Press, 1997.

Green, R. P. H. *The Works of Ausonius*. New York: Oxford University Press, 1991.

Gregarek, H. 1999. "Untersuchungen zur kaiserzeitlichen Idealplastik aus Buntmarmor." *Kölner Jahrbuch für Vor- und Frühgeschichte* 32: 33-284.

Gurval, R. A. *Actium and Augustus: The Politics and Emotions of Civil War*. Ann Arbor: University of Michigan Press, 1998.

Hallett, J. P. "'Over Troubled Water': The Meaning of the Title *Pontifex*." *Transaction of the American Philological Association* 101 (1970): 219-27.

Hardie, P. R. "The Speech of Pythagoras in Ovid *Metamorphoses* 15: Empedoclean *Epos*." *Classical Quarterly* 45, no. 1 (1995): 204-14.

Harrison, E. "Greek Sculptured Coiffures and Ritual Haircuts." In *Early Greek Cult Practice: Proceedings of the Fifth International Symposium at the Swedish Institute at Athens, 26-29 June 1986*, edited by R. Hägg, N. Marinatos, and G. C. Nordquist. Stockholm: Svenska Institutet i Athen, 1988.

Haslam, S. M. *The Historic River: Rivers and Culture Down the Ages.* Cambridge: Cobden of Cambridge Press, 1991.

Heidel, A. *The Babylonian Genesis: The Story of the Creation.* Chicago: University of Chicago Press, 1951.

Herendeen, W. H. *From Landscape to Literature: The River and the Myth of Geography.* Pittsburgh, Penn.: Duquesne University Press, 1986.

Hoffman, D. *Paul Bunyan: Last of the Frontier Demigods.* Lincoln: University of Nebraska Press, 1983.

Hofmann, H. "Ein Aratspapyrus bei Vergil." *Hermes* 113 (1985): 468-80.

Holland, L. A. *Janus and the Bridge.* Papers and Monographs of the American Academy in Rome 21. Rome: American Academy in Rome, 1961.

Hubbard, T. K. "Nature and Art in the Shield of Achilles." *Arion* 2, no. 1 (1992): 16-41.

Isager, S. "The Pride of Halicarnassus: Editio Princeps of an inscription from Salmakis." *Zeitschrift für Papyrologie und Epigraphie* 123 (1998): 1-23.

Jacob, C. "Ecritures du Monde: Points de Vue, Parcours et Catalogues." In *Cartes et Figures de la Terre: Exposition Presentée au Centre George Pompidou de 24 Mai au 17 Novembre 1980.* Paris: Centre Georges Pompidou, Centre de Création Industrielle, 1980.

Jenkins, G. K. *Coinage of Gela.* Berlin: De Gruyter, 1970.

Jones, C. P. *"Graia Pandetur ab Urbe."* *Harvard Studies in Classical Philology* 97 (1995): 233-41.

Kahn, C. H. *The Art and Thought of Heraclitus: An Edition of the Fragments with Translation and Commentary.* New York: Cambridge University Press, 1979.

Kepple, L. R. "Arruns and the Death of Aeneas." *American Journal of Philology* 87 (1976): 344-60.

Kirk, G. S., J. E. Raven, and M. Schofield. *The Presocratic Philosophers: A Critical History with a Selection of Texts.* New York: Cambridge University Press, 1993.

Knox, P. "Wine, Water, and Callimachean Polemics." *Harvard Studies in Classical Philology* 89 (1985): 107-19.

———. *Ovid's Metamorphoses and the Traditions of Augustan Poetry.* Cambridge: Cambridge Philological Society, 1986.

Kraay, C. M. *Archaic and Classical Greek Coins.* Berkeley: University of California Press, 1976.

Kupperman, K. O., ed. *America in European Consciousness, 1493-1750.* Chapel Hill: University of North Carolina Press, 1995.

Lichtheim, M. *Ancient Egyptian Literature Volume II: The New Kingdom.* Berkeley: University of California Press, 1976.

Little, D. A. "The Speech of Pythagoras in *Metamorphoses* 15 and the Structure of the *Metamorphoses*." *Hermes* 98 (1970): 340-60.

Lloyd-Jones, H. "The Pride of Halicarnassus." *Zeitschrift für Papyrologie und Epigraphie* 124 (1999): 1-14.

———. "The Pride of Halicarnassus (*Zeitschrift für Papyrologie und Epigraphie* 124 [1999] 1-14) Corrigenda and Addenda." *Zeitschrift für Papyrologie und Epigraphie* 127 (1999a): 63-65.

Mackenthun, G. *Metaphors of Dispossession: American Beginnings and the Translation of Empire, 1492-1637.* Norman: University of Oklahoma Press, 1997.

Meyboom, P. G. B. *The Nile Mosaic of Palestrina: Early Evidence of Egyptian Religion in Italy.* New York: E. J. Brill, 1995.

Mitchell, W. J. T. "Imperial Landscape." In *Landscape and Power*, edited by W. J. T. Mitchell. Chicago: University of Chicago Press, 1994.

Mussini, E. "La Diffusione dell'Iconografia di Acheloo in Magna Grecia e Sicilia. Tracce per l'Individuazione di un Culto." *Studi Etruschi* 65-68 (2002): 91-119.

Mynors, R. A. B., ed. *Virgil: Georgics.* New York: Oxford University Press, 1990.

Nagy, G. "Comparative Studies in Greek and Indic Meter." *Harvard Studies in Comparative Literature* 33 (1974): 245-52.

————. *Greek Mythology and Poetics*. Ithaca, N.Y.: Cornell University Press, 1990.

————. *Poetry as Performance*. New York: Cambridge University Press, 1996.

Nicolet, C. *Space, Geography, and Politics in the Early Roman Empire*. Ann Arbor: University of Michigan Press, 1991.

Ninck, M. "Die Bedeutung des Wassers im Kult und Leben der Alten." *Philologus* Suppl. 14, Heft 2 (1921): 138-80.

Norden, E. *Die Antike Kunstprosa vom VI. Jahrhundert v. Chr. bis in die Zeit der Renaissance*. Leipzig: B. G. Teubner, 1923.

Northrup, M. D. "Homer's Catalogue of Women." *Ramus* 9 (1980): 150-59.

Ogilvie, R. M. *A Commentary on Livy Books 1-5*. Oxford: Clarendon Press, 1965.

O'Hara, J. J. *Death and the Optimistic Prophecy in Vergil's Aeneid*. Princeton, N.J.: Princeton University Press, 1990.

Östenberg, I. "Demonstrating the Conquest of the World: The Procession of Peoples and Rivers on the Shield of Aeneas and the Triple Triumph of Octavian in 29 B.C." *Opuscula Romana: Annual of the Swedish Institute in Rome* 24 (1999): 155-62.

Ostrowski, J. A. *Personifications of Rivers in Greek and Roman Art*. Warszawa-Krakow: Nakadem Uniwersytetu Jagielloskiego, 1991.

Otis, B. *Ovid as an Epic Poet*. Cambridge: Cambridge University Press, 1966.

Parker, R. *Miasma: Pollution and Purification in Early Greek Religion*. New York: Clarendon Press, 1996.

Parry, A. "Landscape in Greek Poetry." *Yale Classical Studies* 15 (1957): 3-29.

Parry, H. "Ovid's *Metamorphoses*: Violence in a Pastoral Landscape." *Transactions of the American Philological Association* 95 (1964): 268-82.

Powell, B. B. *Classical Myth*. Upper Saddle River, N.J.: Prentice Hall, 2001.

Powell, J. U. *Collectanea Alexandrina: Reliquiae Poetarum Graecorum Aetatis Ptolemaicae, 323-146 A.C., Epicorum, Elegiacorum, Lyricorum, Ethicorum*. Oxford: Clarendon Press, 1925.

Quint, D. *Epic and Empire: Politics and Generic Form from Virgil to Milton.* Princeton, N.J.: Princeton University Press, 1993.

Ramage, N. H. and A. Ramage. *Roman Art: Romulus to Constantine.* Englewood Cliffs, N.J.: Prentice Hall, 1991.

Redfield, J. *Nature and Culture in the Iliad.* Chicago: University of Chicago Press, 1975.

Reinhardt, K. *Parmenides und die Geschichte der griechischen Philosophie.* Frankfurt: V. Klostermann, 1985.

Romm, J. *The Edges of the Earth in Ancient Thought: Geography, Exploration, and Fiction.* Princeton, N.J.: Princeton University Press, 1992.

Ross, D. O. *Backgrounds to Augustan Poetry: Gallus, Elegy, and Rome.* New York: Cambridge University Press, 1975.

Rudhardt, J. *La thème de l'eau primordiale dans la mythologie grècque.* Bern: Franke, 1971.

Russo, C. F. *Scutum: Introduzione, testo critico e commento con traduzione e indici.* Florence: Nuova Italia, 1965.

Schama, S. *Landscape and Memory.* New York: A. A. Knopf, 1995.

Schneider, R. M. *Bunte Barbaren: Orientalenstatuen aus farbigem Marmor in der römischen Repräsentationskunst.* Worms: Wernersche Verlagsgesellschaft, 1986.

Scodel, R. S. and R. F. Thomas. "Virgil and the Euphrates." *American Journal of Philology* 105 (1984): 339.

Segal, C. P. "Gorgias and the Psychology of the Logos." *Harvard Studies in Classical Philology* 66 (1962): 99-155.

———. "Myth and Philosophy in the *Metamorphoses*: Ovid's Augustanism and the Augustan Conclusion of Book XV." *American Journal of Philology* 90 (1969): 257-92.

———. *Singers, Heroes, and Gods in the Odyssey.* Ithaca, N.Y.: Cornell University Press, 1994.

Settis, S., ed. *La colonna Traiana.* Torino: G. Einaudi, 1988.

Shils, E. *Center and Periphery: Essays in Macrosociology*. Chicago: University of Chicago Press, 1975.

Slatkin, L. M. *The Power of Thetis: Allusion and Interpretation in the Iliad*. Berkeley: University of California Press, 1991.

Squatriti, P. *Water and Society in Early Medieval Italy*. New York: Cambridge University Press, 1998.

Taplin, O. "The Shield of Achilles Within the *Iliad*." In *Homer*, edited by I. McAuslan and P. Walcot. New York: Oxford University Press on behalf of the Classical Association, 1998.

Thomas, R. F. *Lands and Peoples in Roman Poetry*. Cambridge: Cambridge Philological Society, 1982.

———. "Callimachus, the *Victoria Berenices*, and Roman Poetry." *Classical Quarterly* n.s. 33 (1983): 92-101.

———. "Virgil's Ecphrastic Centerpieces." *Harvard Studies in Classical Philology* 87 (1983a): 175-84.

———. "From *Recusatio* to Commitment: The Evolution of the Virgilian Program." *Papers of the Liverpool Latin Seminar* 5 (1985): 61-73.

———., ed. *Virgil Georgics*. New York: Cambridge University Press, 1988.

———. "The Old Man Revisited: Memory, Reference, and Genre in Virg. *Georg.* 4,116-48." *Materiali e Discussioni per l'Analisi dei Testi Classici* 29 (1992): 35-70.

Tindall, W. Y. *A Reader's Guide to Finnegans Wake*. New York: Farrar, Strauss and Giroux, 1969.

Toynbee, J. M. C. *Death and Burial in the Roman World*. Ithaca, N.Y.: Cornell University Press, 1971.

Treggiari, S. *Roman Marriage: Iusti Coniuges from the Time of Cicero to the Time of Ulpian*. New York: Oxford University Press, 1993.

Verene, D. P., ed. *Vico and Joyce*. Albany: State University of New York Press, 1987.

Vermeule, E. *Aspects of Death in Early Greek Art and Poetry*. Berkeley: University of California Press, 1979.

Versnel, H. S. *Triumphus: An Inquiry into the Origin, Development, and Meaning of the Roman Triumph.* Leiden: Brill, 1970.

Wallace, P. W. "Hesiod and the Valley of the Muses." *Greek, Roman, and Byzantine Studies* 15 (1974): 5-24.

West, M. L. "Three Presocratic Cosmologies." *Classical Quarterly* 13 (1963): 154-76.

———. "Zum Neuen Goldblättchen aus Hipponion." *Zeitschrift für Papyrologie und Epigraphie* 18 (1975): 229-36.

Whitbread, L. G. *Fulgentius the Mythographer.* Columbus: Ohio State University Press, 1971.

Wilkinson, L. P. *The Georgics of Virgil: A Critical Survey.* London: Cambridge University Press, 1969.

Willcock, M. M., ed. *The Iliad of Homer: Books 1-24.* New York: St. Martin's Press, 1978.

Williams, M. F. *Landscape in the Argonautica of Apollonius Rhodius.* Studien zur klassischen Philologie 63. New York: Peter Lang, 1991.

Williams, R. D., ed. *The Aeneid of Virgil: Books 7-12.* New York: St. Martin's Press, 1987.

Wimmel, W. *Kallimachos in Rom.* Wiesbaden: F. Steiner, 1960.

Zaidman, L. B. and P. S. Pantel. *Religion in the Ancient Greek City,* tr. P. Cartledge. New York: Cambridge University Press, 1992.

Zimmerman, M. and D. Slavitt. *Metamorphoses: A Play.* Evanston, Ill.: Northwestern University Press, 2002.

Index

About the Author

Prudence Jones received her B.A. from Wellesley College and M.A. and Ph.D. from Harvard University. She is an assistant professor at Montclair State University and has also taught at Bryn Mawr College and Rutgers University. In addition to rivers, her research interests include Augustan literature and society, ancient geography, and Cleopatra VII.